What to See

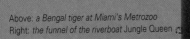

Above: a Bengal tiger at Miami's Metrozoo
Right: the funnel of the riverboat Jungle Queen

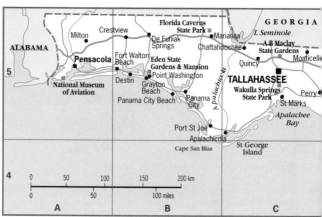

GEORGIA

ALABAMA

Florida Caverns State Park
Crestview
Milton
De Funiak Springs
Marianna
L. Seminole
Chattahoochee
A B Maclay State Gardens
Monticell
Pensacola
Fort Walton Beach
Eden State Gardens & Mansion
Quincy
5
Point Washington
TALLAHASSEE
National Museum of Aviation
Destin
Grayton Beach
Wakulla Springs State Park
Perry
Panama City Beach
Panama City
St Marks
N. palachicola
Port St Joe
Apalachee Bay
Apalachicola
St George Island
Cape San Blas

4
0   50   100   150   200 km
0   50   100 miles

A   B   C

Did you know?

A delightful spot at Coral Gables is the Venetian Pool. Fed by a natural spring, the blue lagoon was carved out of an old stone quarry and landscaped with a sandy beach and Venetian-inspired bridges and changing room buildings. Open daily 15 June– 1 September. Closed Mondays rest of year.

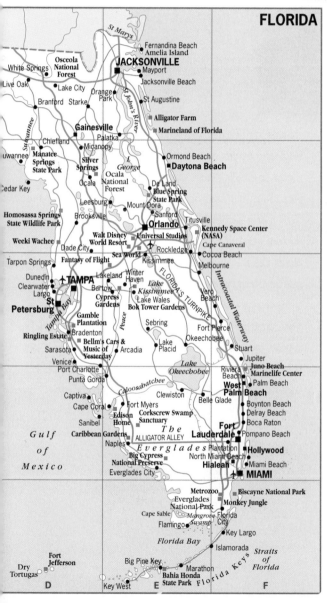

FLORIDA

St Marys

Fernandina Beach
Amelia Island
Osceola
White Springs National **JACKSONVILLE**
Forest ■ Mayport
Live Oak Lake City Jacksonville Beach
Orange
Branford Starke Park ● St Augustine

St John's River

■ **Alligator Farm**
Gainesville Palatka
Chiefland Micanopy ■ **Marineland of Florida**

Manatee Ormond Beach
uwannee Springs **Silver** ● L ● ■ **Daytona Beach**
State Park **Springs** George
Cedar Key Ocala De Land
National Blue Spring
Forest State Park
Leesburg Mount Dora
Homosassa Springs Brooksville Sanford Titusville
State Wildlife Park **Orlando** Kennedy Space Center
Walt Disney Universal Studios (NASA)
Weeki Wachee **World Resort** ● Rockledge Cape Canaveral
Dade City **Sea World** Cocoa Beach
Tarpon Springs **Fantasy of Flight** Kissimmee

FLORIDA'S TURNPIKE

Dunedin **↑TAMPA** Lakeland Winter Melbourne
Clearwater Bartow Haven
Largo Lake Vero
St Cypress Kissimmee Beach
Petersburg **Gardens** Lake Wales
Gamble **Bok Tower Gardens**
Plantation Sebring Fort Pierce
Ringling Estate Bradenton Okeechobee
Bellm's Cars & Lake Stuart
Sarasota Music of Arcadia Placid
Venice Yesterday Jupiter
Port Charlotte Lake Riviera Juno Beach
Punta Gorda Okeechobee Beach **Marinelife Center**
Caloosahatchee **West** Palm Beach
Captiva Clewiston **Palm Beach**
Cape Coral Fort Myers Belle Glade Boynton Beach
Edison **Corkscrew Swamp** Delray Beach
Sanibel Home **Sanctuary** Boca Raton
Caribbean Gardens The **Fort** Pompano Beach
Naples ALLIGATOR ALLEY **Lauderdale**
Everglades Plantation **Hollywood**
Big Cypress North Miami Beach
National Preserve **Hialeah** ●Miami Beach
Everglades City ✈ ■ **MIAMI**

Metrozoo ■ **Biscayne National Park**
Everglades ■ Monkey Jungle
National Park
Cape Sable Mangrove Florida
Flamingo Swamp City
● Key Largo

Florida Bay Islamorada

Fort
Dry **Jefferson** *Straits*
Tortugas *of*
Big Pine Key *Florida*
Marathon
Bahia Honda Florida Keys
Key West State Park

Gulf

of

Mexico

Suwannee

Peace

Intracoastal Waterway

D E F

Miami

Big, brash, and sexy, Miami comes on like a Hollywood starlet displaying her attractions in an enviable tropical setting. The palm trees, the shimmering beaches, the wide blue skies, and the sailboats skimming across glittering Biscayne Bay are just as they should be. The vertiginous downtown skyline serves the joint purpose of sightseeing attraction and a measure of the city's recent success. This is a city on the make and it does not care who knows.

Miami has an intriguingly international flavor. Poised at the gateway to Latin America, there is a touch of salsa in its soul and a large and voluble Cuban community who know how to make good coffee and dine late. Europeans have also made inroads, particularly in SoBe (South Beach), the terminally hip Miami Beach Art Deco District, whose unique brand of cutting edge kitsch has become an international style icon.

> *"Miami's neon glitter and pulse of Broadway are tempered by the languor of the tropics, and time is as negligible as yesterday's weather report. "*
>
> The WPA Guide
> To Florida (1939)

Miami

It is little more than a century since pioneer Julia Tuttle lured Henry Flagler and his railroad south with a bouquet of orange blossom despatched during the devastating 1894–5 Great Freeze in central Florida. Today, the sprawling bayfront metropolis has a population of 2.2 million and ranks as the third most popular city destination in the U.S. after Los Angeles and New York.

Bathed in neon, the impressive NationsBank building towers over downtown Miami

The main resort areas are on Miami Beach, with the Art Deco District in the south, the major hotels in the middle, and more budget-orientated options in the north. On the mainland, downtown is well supplied with executive-style hotels, there are a few upscale choices in Coconut Grove and Coral Lakes, or smart resorts on Key Biscayne, and budget places near the airport. Miami's sights are widespread, with several family-orientated attractions a good 45-minute drive south of downtown. To get the most from a stay of more than a couple of days, a car is helpful.

What to See in Miami

ART DECO DISTRICT (▶ 16, TOP TEN; ▶ 34, WALK)

BASS MUSEUM OF ART
Tucked away in a small grassy park, the Bass is a real treat laid out over two floors of a 1930 art deco building. European old master paintings, drawings, and sculpture from the Renaissance, baroque and rococo periods are augmented by a superb collection of 16th-century Flemish tapestries. There are more modern works and collections of antique furniture and *objets d'art*. Special exhibits focus on the many different strengths of the permanent collections, and the museum hosts a broad-ranging program of visiting exhibitions and weekend cultural events.

✚ 32C3
✉ 2121 Park Avenue, Miami Beach
☎ 305/673 7530
🕐 Tue, Wed, Fri, Sat 10–5, Thu 10–9, Sun 11–5
🚌 G, K, L, S
♿ Good
🎟 Moderate

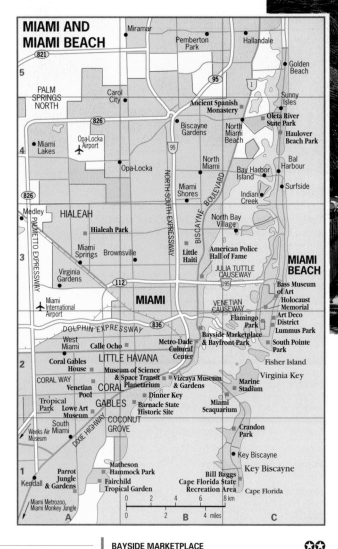

MIAMI AND MIAMI BEACH

- 821
- 95
- 1
- 826
- 95
- 826
- PALMETTO EXPRESSWAY
- NORTH-SOUTH EXPRESSWAY
- BISCAYNE BOULEVARD
- 112
- 836
- DIXIE HIGHWAY

Miramar
Pemberton Park
Hallandale
Golden Beach
PALM SPRINGS NORTH
Carol City
Sunny Isles
Ancient Spanish Monastery
Biscayne Gardens
North Miami Beach
Oleta River State Park
Miami Lakes
Opa-Locka Airport
North Miami
Haulover Beach Park
Opa-Locka
Bay Harbor Island
Bal Harbour
Miami Shores
Indian Creek
Surfside
Medley
HIALEAH
North Bay Village
Hialeah Park
Miami Springs
Brownsville
Little Haiti
American Police Hall of Fame
MIAMI BEACH
Virginia Gardens
JULIA TUTTLE CAUSEWAY
Bass Museum of Art
Miami International Airport
MIAMI
VENETIAN CAUSEWAY
Holocaust Memorial
DOLPHIN EXPRESSWAY
Flamingo Park
Art Deco District
Lummus Park
West Miami
Calle Ocho
Metro-Dade Cultural Center
Bayside Marketplace & Bayfront Park
South Pointe Park
Coral Gables House
LITTLE HAVANA
Museum of Science & Space Transit Planetarium
Vizcaya Museum & Gardens
Fisher Island
CORAL WAY
Venetian Pool
CORAL GABLES
Dinner Key
Marine Stadium
Virginia Key
Tropical Park
Lowe Art Museum
Barnacle State Historic Site
Miami Seaquarium
Weeks Air Museum
South Miami
COCONUT GROVE
Crandon Park
Parrot Jungle & Gardens
Matheson Hammock Park
Key Biscayne
Kendall
Fairchild Tropical Garden
Bill Baggs Cape Florida State Recreation Area
Key Biscayne
Miami Metrozoo, Miami Monkey Jungle
Cape Florida

0   2   4   6   8 km
0   2   4 miles

A   B   C

BAYSIDE MARKETPLACE ●●

A waterfront shopping, dining, and entertainment complex, downtown Bayside is a popular stop on the tourist trail. The open-air mall features around 150 boutiques and gift stores, a Hard Rock Café, a food court, cafés, bars, and restaurants. Free entertainment is provided by wandering street performers and there is live music nightly. Bayside is conveniently accessible by water taxi, and regular Biscayne Bay sightseeing cruises depart from the dock.

- 32B2
- 401 N Biscayne Boulevard
- 305/577 3344
- Mon–Thu 10–10, Fri–Sat 10–11, Sun 11–9
- College/Bayside
- C, S, 16, 48, 95

COCONUT GROVE ✪✪✪

The Grove is one of Miami's oldest and most appealing neighborhoods. Once a byword for Bohemian living, recently the neighborhood has been shaken from its reverie by an influx of bright young things, and the busy intersection of Grand Avenue and Main Highway has been inundated with chic shops and galleries, sidewalk cafés and the CocoWalk shopping center. However, the atmosphere is still relaxed and friendly and it is a great place to hang out. There are historic homes in the pioneer **Barnacle State Historic Site**, hidden in a hardwood hammock on the water, and palatial Vizcaya (➤ 37). The 1920s Coconut Grove Playhouse is also worth visiting for its elaborate Spanish-style stucco facade and reputation as a leading local repertory theater.

CORAL GABLES ✪✪

A gracious product of the 1920s land boom, the leafy residential enclave of Coral Gables is deemed grand enough to have its own driving tour. Maps are available from City Hall, on Miracle Mile, and stops along the way include the fabulous Biltmore Hotel (➤ 100) and developer George Merrick's bijou "Villages." These little groups of homes were built in a variety of eye-catching architectural styles, from Chinese to Dutch Colonial.

🔲 32A1
🍴 Cafés/restaurants ($–$$$)
🚌 12, 24, 48
❓ Goombay Festival, Jun

Barnacle State Historic Site
✉ 3485 Main Highway
☎ 305/448 9445
🕐 Fri–Sun, tours at 10, 11:30, 1, 2:30
♿ Limited
💲 Cheap

🔲 32A2
🍴 Cafés/restaurants ($–$$$)
🚌 24, 72

Above: *lively Miamarina in Bayside Marketplace*

33

A Walk Around South Beach

Distance
Just over 2½ miles to Bass Museum; 4-mile circuit to Welcome Center

Time
2 hours with coffee stops and browsing. Add at least an hour for a visit to the museum

Start/end point
Ocean Drive
✚ 32C2
🚍 K, S, M, C

Lunch
Wolfie's ($)
✉ 2038 Collins Avenue
☎ 305/538 6626

The haunting Holocaust Memorial is set around a tranquil lily pond

This walk starts at the Art Deco Welcome Center (➤ 16), and heads north on Ocean Drive to 15th Street, past a showcase array of delectable deco delights.

Turn left on 15th, left on Collins Avenue, doubling back for 200yds to a right turn onto Espanola Way.

A pretty little Mediterranean pastiche, between Drexel and Washington Avenues, Espanola is a good place to stop for coffee and window shopping.

Continue westward on Espanola Way to Pennsylvania Avenue. Turn right and head north to Lincoln Road; turn left.

Dozens of galleries, boutiques, and café-restaurants have gravitated to the pedestrian-zoned Lincoln Road Mall. Art deco highlights include the restored Lincoln Theatre and the Sterling Building with its glass-block headband (spectacular at night).

Head north on Meridian Avenue for three-and-a-half blocks to the Holocaust Memorial.

The centerpiece of this enormously moving memorial is a giant bronze arm reaching skyward from a seething mass of doomed humanity. Victims' names are inscribed on a memorial wall and the horror of the Holocaust is described in words and pictures.

Double back to 19th Street and turn left alongside the Convention Center parking lot. At the end of the street turn left and look for the canal-side footpath on the right, which rejoins Washington Avenue. Cross Washington on to 21st Street. After a block-and-a-half, the Bass Museum (➤ 31) will be found on the left. Turn right along Collins Avenue, by Wolfie's famous deli restaurant, and head south, back toward Ocean Drive, passing on the way some of Miami Beach's finest hotels.

FAIRCHILD TROPICAL GARDEN

These magnificent botanical gardens, the largest in the U.S., consist of an 83-acre tract of lawns and lakes, hardwood hammocks, and miniature rainforest. The palm collection is one of the largest in the world, and there are tropical blooms and a specialist Rare Plant House. A narrated streetcar tour sets the scene; then you are on your own to explore the trails through coastal mangrove and Everglades areas. Next to the Fairchild, Matheson Hammock Park is a good place to swim and enjoy a picnic.

🚶 32A1
✉ 10901 Old Cutler Road, Coral Gables
☎ 305/667 1651
🕐 Daily 9:30–4:30
🍴 Café ($)
🚌 65
♿ Very good
💲 Moderate

KEY BISCAYNE 🔵🔵

Reached by the Rickenbacker Causeway (toll), which affords a fantastic view of downtown Miami, Key Biscayne presents a choice of good beaches. The broad, 5-mile stretch of public beach at Crandon Park is understandably popular, but the **Bill Baggs Cape Florida State Recreation Area** has considerably more to offer for a day out. The 500-acre park was badly hit by Hurricane Andrew in 1992, but the bicycling and walking trails, boardwalks, and barbecue grills have all been restored or replaced. Fishing is another popular pastime, and the 1845 Cape Florida lighthouse is also open to the public.

🚶 32C1

Bill Baggs Cape Florida State Recreation Area
✉ 1200 S Crandon Boulevard
☎ 305/361 5811
🕐 Daily 8AM–sunset
🍴 Snack concessions ($)
♿ Good
💲 Cheap

MIAMI BEACH 🔵🔵🔵

Miami Beach's golden shores are divided up into a number of sections each patronized by a different clientele. The southern reaches around South Pointe Park are popular with surfers and Cuban families. The SoBe (South Beach) section between 5th and 21st Streets is the most hip and crowded, with a gay focus around 12th Street. North of 21st Street, the crowd is more family-orientated, though nude bathing is legal in the northern section of Haulover Park.

🚶 32C3
✉ Ocean Drive and cross-streets off Collins Avenue. Boardwalk from 21st Street to 46th Street
🚌 K, S, M, C

Miami's art deco hotels make a pleasing backdrop to the busy beaches

MIAMI METROZOO ✪✪✪
This huge and attractively laid out zoo features more than 800 animals from 190 species, most of them housed in spacious natural habitat enclosures. The monorail is a good way to get an overview of what is on offer; then be sure to stop off at the Bengal tigers, the koalas, the cute Himalayan black bears and pygmy hippos, and the gorillas. There are wildlife shows throughout the day, and Dr. Wilde's Wonders of Tropical America offers activities for children.

✚ 29F1
✉ 12400 SW 152nd Street, South Miami
☎ 305/251 0400
🕐 Daily 9:30–5:30

MIAMI SEAQUARIUM ✪✪
Performances by Lolita the killer whale, Flipper the dolphin, and Salty the sea lion are among the highlights at this venerable sealife attraction. In between the shows and the popular Shark Channel presentations, there are dozens of aquarium displays to inspect, petting experiences, and the gently educational manatee exhibit. The Seaquarium is a leading marine research center and operates a Marine Mammal Rescue Team which cares for injured manatees. These huge but gentle creatures that live in shallow waters are often the victims of boat propellers.

✚ 32C2
✉ 4400 Rickenbacker Causeway, Virginia Key (Key Biscayne)
☎ 305/361 5705
🕐 Daily 9:30–5
🍴 Various concessions and cafés ($–$$)
🚍 B
♿ Very good
💷 Expensive

MONKEY JUNGLE ✪
Monkey Jungle's special appeal is the free-roaming macaque monkey colony released by Joe DuMond in 1933. Instead of locking up the monkeys at his behavioral research facility turned sightseeing attraction, DuMond decided to cage the visitors by enclosing boardwalk trails through the woodlands. While the descendants of the original six monkeys now scamper about at liberty, most of the other inhabitants, from gibbons and colobus monkeys to tiny tamarins, are securely caged. Monkey programs and feeding times are scheduled throughout the day.

✚ 29F1
✉ 14805 SW 216th Street, South Miami
☎ 305/235 1611
🕐 Daily 9:30–5
🍴 Snack bar ($)
♿ Very good
💷 Expensive

Above: *the immensely powerful Bengal tiger*

MUSEUM OF SCIENCE AND SPACE TRANSIT PLANETARIUM ✪✪✪
A first-class science museum with a raft of imaginative interactive exhibits, this is the place to sample virtual reality basketball, climb a rock wall or enjoy the traveling Smithsonian Exhibitions program. The natural world is represented in the coral reef and Everglades displays and there is a Wildlife Center where rescued birds and reptiles are rehabilitated for release back into their natural habitats. Regular astronomical presentations take place in the Space Transit Planetarium.

✚ 32B2
✉ 3280 S Miami Avenue, Coconut Grove
☎ 305/646 4200
🕐 Daily 10–6
🍴 Café ($)
🚇 Metrorail Vizcaya
🚍 48
♿ Very good
💷 Moderate

PARROT JUNGLE ISLAND

Over 3,000 exotic animals and 500 species of plants have an excellent jungle home on 18.6-acre Watson Island between downtown Miami and South Beach. The parrots reside at a re-creation of the cliffs of Manu, a natural habitat in Peru, while the pink flamingos made famous in the credits to the popular 1980s television series *Miami Vice* can also be found here. There's an Everglades habitat, where pride of place is taken by a rare albino alligator, and Jungle Theater plays host to regular animal shows.

- 32C2
- 1111 Parrot Jungle Trail, off 395, Miami Beach
- 305/2 JUNGLE
- Daily 10–6
- Lakeside Café ($)
- Good
- Expensive

VIZCAYA MUSEUM AND GARDENS

Millionaire industrialist James Deering had this splendid Italian Renaissance-style villa constructed as a winter residence in 1914–16. Together with his architect, F. Burrell Hoffman Jr., and designer, Paul Chalfin, Deering trawled Europe for the 15th- to 19th-century antiques that furnish the Renaissance dining room, the rococo salon, and the English-style Adams Library. The formal gardens that lead down to Biscayne Bay are peopled by a wealth of statuary and enclosed by native hardwood trees, while the dock is styled after a Venetian water landing and is protected by a stone gondola.

- 32B2
- 3251 S Miami Avenue, Coconut Grove
- 305/250 9133
- Daily 9:30–5
- Vizcaya Café ($–$$)
- Metrorail Vizcaya
- 48
- Reasonable
- Moderate

Vizcaya mansion sits amid striking formal gardens

Southern Florida & the Florida Keys

Less than a century ago, southern Florida was pioneer territory dominated by the mysterious, waterlogged expanses of the Everglades. It is hard to believe today, for this is Florida's most populous and most visited tourist heartland.

Bordering the beleaguered Everglades, the Gold Coast unfurls seamlessly north from Miami to West Palm Beach, combining the accessible attractions of Fort Lauderdale with more exclusive haunts such as Boca Raton and Palm Beach. The southern Gulf coast is only slightly less developed between the twin poles of upscale Naples and Fort Myers. The latter, with a wide range of sightseeing possibilities and the lovely barrier islands of Sanibel and Captiva (➤ 24), makes an especially good family vacation destination.

Trailing off toward the tropics, the Florida Keys provide a somewhat different brand of hospitality and a relaxed style that captures the hearts of many visitors.

> *"Florida…does beguile and gratify me – giving me my first and last (evidently) sense of the tropics…"*
>
> HENRY JAMES
> *Letter to Edmund Gosse*
> (1905)

───────●───────

The Overseas Highway links the Florida Keys

Mizner Park, an impressive shopping mall in Boca Raton

🏠 29F1
✉ 9700 SW 328th Street, Homestead
☎ 305/230 1100
🕐 Daily 8–5:30; Visitor Center daily 8:30–5
♿ Good
👝 Cheap

🏠 29F2
❓ Boca Festival Days, Aug

Boca Raton Museum of Art
✉ 501 Mizner Park
☎ 561/392 2500
🕐 Tue, Thu, Sat 10–5, Wed, Fri 10–9, Sun 12–5
♿ Very good
👝 Cheap

What to See in Southern Florida and the Florida Keys

BISCAYNE NATIONAL PARK ⭐

A 181,500-acre park with a surprising difference, namely that over 96 percent of this national preserve is under water. It protects a live coral reef, which is home to more than 200 varieties of tropical fish, and an 18-mile-long chain of unspoiled island keys notable for marine and bird life. Snorkel and dive trips can be arranged from the Visitor Center at Convoy Point and glass-bottomed boat tours offer an alternative window on the underwater world.

BOCA RATON ⭐⭐

The well-heeled Gold Coast city of Boca Raton is a vision of strawberry ice-cream pink mansions and malls inspired by its Roaring Twenties founder Addison Mizner (▶ 21), who planned to make it the "greatest resort in the world". The land boom crash of 1926 put paid to his grandiose scheme, but several Mizner creations survive, including the exclusive Boca Raton Resort and Club.

Boca has the aura of a giant country club offering golf, tennis, watersports, and some superb beach parks. The two most exclusive (and pink) shopping malls are the Royal Palm Plaza and Mizner Park, with their classy little boutiques and galleries. Art lovers also have a treat in store at the **Boca Raton Museum of Art**, which features frequently changing exhibitions and the Mayers Collection of works by 19th- and 20th-century artists including Degas, Picasso, and Matisse, as well as a sculpture garden.

CAPTIVA ISLAND (▶ 24, TOP TEN)

Above: *the anhinga, denizen of the Everglades*

CORKSCREW SWAMP SANCTUARY ✪✪✪

The National Audubon Society first posted guards on Corkscrew Swamp in 1912 to protect herons and egrets from plume hunters. The 11,000-acre sanctuary is now renowned for its superb bird life (► 13) and the nation's largest stand of giant bald cypress trees. An excellent 2¼-mile boardwalk trail traverses the shadowy swamp woodlands, where ancient cypress trees tower up to 130ft high. Some of these rare survivors of the 1940s and 50s Everglades logging booms are over 500 years old. Look for wading birds feeding on the floating lettuce lakes and there may be a glimpse of an alligator or otters.

✚ 29E2

✉ 375 Sanctuary Road, West Naples, (exit 111 on 175)

☎ 941/348 9151

🕐 Daily 12 Apr–30 Sep 7–7:30 (rest of year 7–5:30)

♿ Good

✋ Moderate

EVERGLADES NATIONAL PARK ✪✪

The base of the Florida peninsula is like a giant sieve slowly draining the Everglades into the Gulf of Mexico through the maze of the Ten Thousand Islands. The "river of grass" begins its journey to the sea at Lake Okeechobee and flows southwest into the 1½ million-acre national park, which is a mere fifth of the Everglades' actual size.

There are three entrances to the park, with the main visitor center on the eastern side, 10 miles west of Florida City. Here, a variety of short boardwalk trails venture into the sea of sawgrass dotted with island hammocks, which offer the best chance of spotting the local flora and fauna (► 12–13), there are ranger-led walks and boat rentals at the Flamingo Marina throughout the year from Royal Palm Visitor Center, west of the main entrance. Tram tours depart from the northern Shark Valley entrance (► 108), on US41, 35 miles west of Miami. Canoe rentals and tours are available from the western Gulf Coast Visitor Center, near Everglades City.

✚ 29E1

✉ Main Visitor Center, SR9336 (W of US1)

☎ 305/242 7700

🕐 Daily 8–5

🍴 Flamingo ($–$$)

♿ Reasonable

✋ Cheap (tickets valid for 7 days)

Gulf Coast Visitor Center

✉ CR29, Everglades City

☎ 941/695 3311

🕐 Daily 7:30–5 in winter, reduced in summer

Above left: *the boardwalk trail at Corkscrew Swamp Sanctuary*

The Gold Coast

A leisurely day trip with time for sightseeing, this drive follows the Gold Coast north between Fort Lauderdale and Palm Beach.

Begin at the intersection of Sunrise Boulevard and South Ocean Boulevard (A1A), and head north on A1A for 14 miles to the intersection with Camino Real in Boca Raton. Turn left, passing the Boca Raton Resort and Country Club, then turn right on Federal Highway. Cross Palmetto Park Road and turn right into Mizner Park.

Window shopping at Mizner Park is a favorite pastime in ostentatious Boca Raton (➤ 40).

Return to Palmetto Park Road. For the direct route to Palm Beach, turn left and rejoin A1A. For an interesting detour, turn right. At Powerline Road (4½ miles), turn right and head north for 5¾ miles to the entrance to the Morikami Museum and Japanese Gardens.

Chic boutiques are a feature of pink-hued Mizner Park

Set in peaceful formal gardens, Japanese cultural exhibits and artifacts are displayed in the Yamoto-kan villa and museum galleries.

Distance
50 miles

Time
2 hours. A day trip with stops

Start point
Fort Lauderdale
✚ 29F2

End point
Palm Beach
✚ 29F2

Lunch
Mark's at the Park ($)
✉ Mizner Park, Boca Raton
☎ 561/395 0770

Turn left out of the Morikami. At the intersection with Atlantic Avenue/SR806, turn right and continue through Deerfield Beach. Rejoin A1A north for 15 miles to a junction outside Palm Beach. Bear right for A1A N on South Ocean Boulevard. Just under a mile later, keep right on Ocean Boulevard for just over a mile, then turn left on to Worth Avenue.

Worth Avenue is the gold-plated heart of downtown Palm Beach (➤ 21).

For a fast return to Fort Lauderdale, take Royal Palm Way (five blocks north of Worth) across to West Palm Beach and follow signs for I-95.

FORT LAUDERDALE ✪✪

The largest city on the Gold Coast, Fort Lauderdale combines with ease its dual roles of thriving business and cultural center and popular beach resort. The namesake fort was founded on the New River in 1838, during the Second Seminole War, and the small settlement developed into a busy trading post before the arrival of the railroad. A special feature of the downtown district is the "Venice of America," a network of canals and islands dredged in the 1920s, which boasts some of the city's most desirable waterfront properties; these are best viewed from one of the regular sightseeing cruises.

The New River meanders through the city center conveniently linking a handful of historic sites and modern cultural landmarks with the 1½-mile Riverwalk. This landscaped route along the north bank begins at the turn-of-the-19th-century **Stranahan House**, the oldest surviving house in town. The pioneering Stranahans used to entertain railroad baron Henry Flagler in their heart pine parlor, and the interior faithfully re-creates a Florida home of 1913–15. There is a small local history museum laid out in a former inn in the Old Fort Lauderdale district, and the Riverwalk ends at the Broward Center for Performing Arts.

Fort Lauderdale's main shopping and dining district is Las Olas Boulevard, an attractive, tree-shaded street that leads to the **Museum of Art**. The striking museum building is a fitting showcase for extensive collections of 19th- and 20th-century European and American art and visiting exhibitions. Nearby, the **Museum of Discovery and Science** is one of Florida's finest, with a spectacular range of exhibits, interactive displays, and an IMAX cinema.

✚ 29F2
↔ Butterfly World (► 108)
❓ Fort Lauderdale Boat Show, Oct

Stranahan House
✉ 335 E Las Olas Boulevard (at SE 6th Avenue)
☎ 954/524 4736
🕐 Wed–Sat 10–3, Sun 1–3
♿ Limited
💰 Cheap

Museum of Art
✉ 1 E Las Olas Boulevard
☎ 954/525 5500
🕐 Mon, Wed, Fri–Sun 11–7, Thu 11–9
♿ Very good
💰 Moderate

Museum of Discovery and Science
✉ 401 SW 2nd Street
☎ 954/467 6637
🕐 Mon–Sat 10–5, Sun 12–6
🍴 Subway Café ($)
♿ Very good
💰 Moderate

Stranahan House was, in its time, considered to be the height of luxury

Bonnet House

⊠ 900 N Birch Road

☎ 954/563 5393

🕐 Tue–Sat 10–4, Sun 12–4.
Last tour 2:30

▥ Moderate

*Above: the Jungle Queen
offers day and evening
cruises on New River*

➕ 29E2

↔ Sanibel and Captiva
Islands

**Edison Winter Home and
Ford Winter Home**

⊠ 2350 McGregor
Boulevard

☎ 239/334 7419

🕐 Mon–Sat 9–4, Sun 12–4

♿ Good

▥ Moderate

Hidden from view by hardwood hammock behind Fort Lauderdale's sandy beach, the **Bonnet House** is a delightful Old Florida relic. The two-story plantation-style house was built by artist Frederic Bartlett in 1920 and the interior is a wonderfully eccentric work of art covered in murals, canvasses, and decorations fashioned out of beachcombing treasures. In the gardens, black and white Australian swans paddle about a miniature lake flanked by the yellow bonnet lilies after which the house is named.

South along the oceanfront, the "Yachting Capital of the World" has its HQ at the Bahia Mar marina, where the *Jungle Queen* riverboat departs for New River cruises. Ocean-going voyages set out from Port Everglades, the second largest cruise ship terminal in the world.

FORT MYERS ⭐⭐

Thomas Alva Edison put Fort Myers on the map back in the 1880s, when the great inventor built himself a winter home in town and planted the first stretch of palms along McGregor Boulevard. Fort Myers now likes to call itself the "City of Palms" and makes a pleasantly relaxed vacation resort with a family-orientated beach annexe and a good selection of sightseeing attractions in and around town.

The **Edison Winter Home** and the **Ford Winter Home** next door, built by Edison's motoring magnate friend Henry Ford, are the most visited sights on the local tourist trail. Visits to the Edison home include a tour of the laboratory, which is packed with examples of the great man's inventions, from the phonograph to miner's lamps. Take time to explore the gardens too, which are planted with a great variety of rare and exotic plants that were collected by Edison while wearing his expert horticulturist hat.

Junior scientists will have a field day at the colorful and entertaining **Imaginarium Hands On Museum and Aquarium** with its impressive store of interactive games and gadgets, saltwater and freshwater aquariums, and a movie theater presenting 3-D film shows. At the **Calusa Nature Center and Planetarium** getting to grips with Florida's native flora and fauna is the name of the game. In addition to snake and alligator presentations, there are bugs, lizards, and touch exhibits, plus nature trails and the Audubon Aviary, a rescue and rehabilitation unit for injured birds.

A short drive east of town, **Manatee World** is a non-captive haven for manatees. In winter, daily boat tours afford a prime view of the animals basking in the warm waters, and there are exhibits to view year round. For animal-spotting with a bit more bite, make tracks for **Babcock Wilderness Adventures** and a bumpy swamp buggy ride around the vast Crescent B Ranch—the tour guides are trained naturalists. As well as bison, quarter horses, and Senepol cattle, the ranch is inhabited by wild alligators, hogs, deer, and turkeys. The buggies also venture into 10,000-acre Telegraph Swamp, where a boardwalk trail leads to a panther enclosure.

Imaginarium Hands On Museum and Aquarium

- ⊠ 2000 Cranford Avenue
- ☎ 941/337 3332
- 🕐 Tue–Sat 10–5, Sun 12–5
- 🍽 Imagateria Café ($)
- ♿ Very good
- 🎫 Moderate

Calusa Nature Center and Planetarium

- ⊠ 3450 Ortiz Avenue
- ☎ 941/275 3435
- 🕐 Mon–Sat 9–5, Sun 11–5
- ♿ Limited
- 🎫 Cheap

Manatee World

- ⊠ 5605 Palm Beach Blvd, SR80 (1.5 miles E of I-75/Exit 25)
- ☎ 941/432 2004
- 🕐 Daily 8–5 (summer 8–8)
- ♿ Good
- 🎫 Moderate

Babcock Wilderness Adventures

- ⊠ 800 SR31 (9½ miles N of SR78), Punto Gorda
- ☎ 1-800 500 5583
- 🕐 Daily, Nov–Apr 9–3; May–Oct mornings only
- 🎫 Expensive
- ❓ Reservations essential

Comfortable wicker armchairs furnish Thomas Edison's home in Fort Myers

Cafés/restaurants ($–$$)
Sport fishing tournaments throughout the year. For information ☎ 305/872 2233

Theater of the Sea
✉ 84721 Overseas Highway, Mile Marker 84.5
☎ 305/664 2431
🕐 Daily 9:30–4
♿ Good
💲 Expensive

29F1
Cafés/restaurants ($–$$$)
Island Jubilee, Nov

John Pennekamp Coral Reef State Park
✉ Mile Marker 102.5
☎ 305/451 1202
🕐 Daily 8–5
♿ Good
💲 Cheap

Florida Keys Wild Bird Center
✉ Mile Marker 93.6
☎ 305/852 4486
🕐 Daily dawn–dusk
♿ Fair
💲 Donation

ISLAMORADA

The self-styled "Sport Fishing Capital of the World," Islamorada consists of a clutch of small islands with a concentration of marinas and Florida's second oldest marine park. Charter boats offer half- and full-day expeditions to the rich Gulf Stream fishing grounds. Local dive operators also do good business and there are trips to the uninhabited island preserves of Indian and Lignumvitae Keys from Lower Matecumbe Key.

Sea lion and dolphin shows are on the bill at the **Theater of the Sea**. This old-style attraction includes all the usual shark encounters and touch tanks, and has added a Dolphin Adventure program which allows visitors to swim with captive dolphins. Understandably popular, the dolphin swim requires reservations (➤ 112).

KEY LARGO

Key Largo ("long island" to the early Spanish explorers) is the largest of the Florida Keys, and a lively resort within easy striking distance of Miami. The island makes a great base for divers, who can explore the depths of the magnificent **John Pennekamp Coral Reef State Park**, which extends for over 3 miles out to sea across the living coral reef. Snorkeling and dive trips, equipment and canoe rental, and a dive school are all available, and there are a range of glass-bottomed boat trips, aquariums in the visitor center, and walking trails on the land-based portion of the park.

Local birdlife is showcased at the **Florida Keys Wild Bird Center** on the neighboring island of Tavernier. This

The dazzling white sands of Bahia Honda State Park are backed by dense tropical forest

rescue and rehabilitation facility has a boardwalk trail past enclosures for hawks, ospreys, cormorants, and pelicans. There are also birdwatching hides overlooking a salt pond where herons and roseate spoonbills come to feed.

KEY WEST (► 18–19, TOP TEN)

LOWER KEYS   ⭐⭐

South of the minor miracle of the Seven Mile Bridge (in reality 110yds short of seven miles), the Lower Keys are less developed than their northern counterparts. Just across the bridge, **Bahia Honda State Park** is one of the finest natural beaches in the Keys and a regular contender in any list of the nation's top ten beaches. Watersports concessions rent out equipment and snorkels, and behind the white sand shore there are walking trails through tropical forest, where several rare trees and plants can be seen.

The other top attraction in this area is the **National Key Deer Refuge**, centered on Big Pine Key. The deer here are pint-sized relatives of the Virginia white-tailed deer and are best spotted in the early morning and evening. Key Deer Boulevard (Mile Marker 30.5) leads to Blue Hole, a freshwater lagoon in an old limestone quarry. Wading birds gather here to feed, and alligators and turtles occasionally put in an appearance. A little farther down the road, Watson's Nature Trail leads off into the forested heart of the refuge.

🚩 29E1

Bahia Honda State Park
✉ Mile Marker 37
☎ 305/872 2353
🕐 Daily 8–sunset
♿ Good
💰 Cheap

National Key Deer Refuge
✉ Refuge Headquarters, 28950 Watson Blvd, Big Pine Key
☎ 305/872 2239
🕐 Refuge, open site; Headquarters, Mon–Fri 8–5
💰 Free

Did you know ?

Dolphin encounter programs are a special feature of the Florida Keys, offering visitors a chance to swim with these highly intelligent and friendly mammals. Several dolphin research centers and the Theater of the Sea offer dolphin encounters (► 112). Reservations (up to two months ahead) are essential.

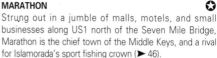

29E1
Cafés/restaurants ($–$$$)

Pigeon Key
Visitor Center at Mile Marker 47
305/743 5999
Daily 10–5
Good
Moderate

29E2
Cafés/restaurants ($–$$$)
Corkscrew Swamp (► 41)

Caribbean Gardens
1590 Goodlette-Frank Road
239/262 5409
Daily 9:30–5:30
Good
Expensive

Facing page: Norton Museum of Art attracts renowned touring exhibitions
Below: a Yellow Cab in the chic Old Naples shopping district

MARATHON ✪

Strung out in a jumble of malls, motels, and small businesses along US1 north of the Seven Mile Bridge, Marathon is the chief town of the Middle Keys, and a rival for Islamorada's sport fishing crown (► 46).

Another good reason to visit Marathon is the Museum of Natural History of the Florida Keys (► 108). Also, the Old Seven Mile Bridge (which doubles as the World's Longest Fishing Pier) gives access to **Pigeon Key**, a former construction workers' camp from the Flagler era recently restored as a National Historic District.

NAPLES ✪✪

A relaxing, small resort city on the Gulf of Mexico, Naples has beautiful beaches, an attractively restored historic shopping and restaurant district in Third Street South, a thriving Center for the Arts and more than 50 championship golf courses.

Naples lies close enough to the Everglades to make a day trip to the national park's western entrance near Everglades City (► 41). Closer to home, visitors to the Naples Nature Center can take to the water on a narrated boat ride, sample woodland nature trails and drop in at the Wildlife Rehabilitation Center, which tends over 1,600 native bird and animal casualties a year.

There are even more exotic beasts in store at **Caribbean Gardens**, a popular zoological park with a special interest in big cats. Daily shows put a selection of lions, tigers, leopards, and cougars through their paces. Many of the animals are the result of the park's successful captive breeding programs.

PALM BEACH (▶ 21, TOP TEN; ▶ 42, DRIVE)

SANIBEL ISLAND (▶ 24, TOP TEN)

WEST PALM BEACH ✪

The high-rise downtown heart of West Palm Beach faces monied and manicured Palm Beach across the Intracoastal Waterway. While the super-rich cavort in the oceanfront resort, West Palm Beach takes care of business and provides a selection of shopping, cultural attractions, and sight-seeing opportunities.

The city's pride and joy is the **Norton Museum of Art,** one of the most important art museums in the southeastern U.S. Built around the collections of steel magnate Ralph Norton (1875–1953), the museum is particularly strong on French Impressionist and Post-Impressionist works (Monet, Matisse, Renoir, Gauguin, Chagall) and 20th-century American art (Hopper, O'Keefe, Pollock), and has a stunning collection of Chinese ceramics, bronzes, and jade carvings.

There are several good outings for children. For "hands-on" interactive fun, the South Florida Science Museum is a big hit. Sparky electricity displays, booming sound waves, and a mini tornado are among the treats on offer. Hands-off is the best way to approach the **Lion Country Safari,** a two-part wildlife park that provides some very close encounters with lions, elephants, rhinos, and giraffes in the 500-acre drive-through African safari section. In the Safari World Park next door there are more animals, fairground rides, lagoon cruises, and a nature trail.

✚ 29F2
↔ Palm Beach Zoo at Dreher Park (▶ 108)
❓ SunFest, Apr–May; Japanese Bon Festival, Aug

Norton Museum of Art
✉ 1451 S Olive Avenue
☎ 561/832 5196
🕐 Tue–Sat 10–5, Sun 1–5 (also Mon Nov–Apr)
♿ Very good
💲 Cheap

Lion Country Safari
✉ W Southern Boulevard/ SR80 (17 miles W of I-95)
☎ 561/793 1084
🕐 Daily 9:30–5:30
♿ Good
💲 Expensive

Did you know ?

During the December to April winter social season, polo is a popular Gold Coast sporting event. The sport draws a host of celebrity fans from Hollywood stars to royalty, and anyone can rub shoulders with them for the inexpensive price of a ticket (▶ 113).

Central Florida

Central Florida's very first theme park was housed in an Orlando fruit-packing warehouse, which had been converted into a skating rink during the icy winter of 1894–5. Leisure attractions have become rather more sophisticated of late (and are rarely as cold), and since the arrival of Walt Disney World, Orlando has been the undisputed gateway to theme park heaven.

Though it is easy for theme park addicts not to venture further afield, visitors in need of a reality check will find that central Florida has much more to offer. Sporting opportunities and state preserves abound, and there are country towns and beach resorts an easy day trip away.

An hour's drive east of Orlando, sea turtles nest on the beach in the shadow of the Kennedy Space Center, one of the state's top attractions. To the west, the cities of St. Petersburg and Tampa offer an irresistible combination of notable sightseeing attractions and superb beaches.

> *"Central Florida—a study in reality suspension, brought to your imagination by the nation's finest fantasy makers."*
>
> FLORIDA TOURIST BOARD

———•———

The dolphin statue in Sarasota's marina complex

A Walk Around Historic Bok Sanctuary

Distance
¾ mile

Time
1½ hours with plenty of stops

Start/end point
Historic Bok Sanctuary
✚ 29E3
✉ CR17-A, 3 miles N of
Lake Wales
☎ 863/676 1408
🕐 Daily 8–6
♿ Good
👣 Moderate

Lunch
Garden Restaurant ($)
✉ Historic Bok Sanctuary
☎ 863/676 1408

*The famous tower,
rising out of pretty
woodland gardens*

These lovely woodland gardens make a relaxing break all year, but they are at the height of their beauty during the cooler winter and spring months. The gardens were founded by Dutch immigrant and philanthropist Edward Bok in the 1920s, and formally opened at a dedication ceremony attended by President Calvin Coolidge in 1929.

From the Visitor Center, take the path that leads up past the dedication plaque and around the White Garden to the Carillon Tower.

The 205ft tower, built of Georgia marble and coquina rock, is adorned with art deco carvings depicting Florida wildlife, and houses the famous 57-bell carillon. Listen out for the clock chimes every half hour, and try to time your visit to coincide with the daily recital at 3PM.

Walk around behind the Carillon Tower to reach the Sunset Overlook.

The Overlook sits at the modest peak of Iron Mountain (298ft), the highest point on the Florida peninsula.

Continue downhill and into the woods on North Walk.

Beneath hanging curtains of Spanish moss, camellias (Nov–Mar), azaleas (Dec–Apr), and other flowering trees and shrubs fill the woodlands with color. Off Mockingbird Walk, Pinewood House and Gardens are open for occasional tours (telephone for details). The romantic Mediterranean Revival-style house was built in 1931 and sits in 7 acres of picturesque lawn. At the bottom of the hill, on Pine Ridge Trail, there is a birdwatching hide by a small pond. More than 126 bird species have been recorded in the gardens.

Return to the Visitor Center along Woodland Walk.

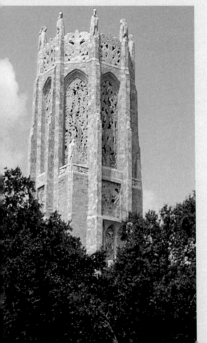

What to See in Central Florida

BLUE SPRING STATE PARK ⊙⊙
This attractive wooded park on the banks of the St. Johns River is one of the best places to see wild manatees in central Florida. During the winter months (Nov–Mar), manatees leave the cool St. Johns River and gather here to bask in the warm waters produced from the turquoise blue depths of the park's namesake artesian spring at a constant 72°F. The spring head is a popular swimming hole and dive site. There are also woodland trails, boat trips, and kayaks for rent.

CYPRESS GARDENS ADVENTURE PARK ⊙⊙
Closed at the time of going to press, Cypress Gardens is due to reopen in summer 2004. The traditional attractions of a fine lakeside setting, water-ski shows, and lush horticultural displays are planned to be augmented by roller coasters and waterpark rides. Contact the website in the panel for up-to-date information.

FANTASY OF FLIGHT ⊙⊙
A major aviation museum between Orlando and Tampa, Fantasy of Flight combines historic aircraft exhibits with state-of-the-art simulator rides. Scale models and authentic aircraft trace the history of flight from the Wright brothers and daredevil antics of 1920s circus barnstormers through to fighter aircraft from World War II and beyond. The Fightertown Flight Simulators put visitors in the hot seat of a B17 Flying Fortress for a stomach-churning mission into enemy territory and an aerial dogfight over the Pacific. If you want to take to the skies yourself, you can reserve a flight in an open cockpit biplane.

29E4
2100 W French Avenue, Orange City
904/775 3663
Daily 8–sunset
Good
Cheap

Below: *dramatic dioramas at Fantasy of Flight*

www.cypressgardens.com
29E3
SR540 W, Winter Haven
For further information contact website above

29E3
SR559, Polk City
941/984 3500
Daily 9–5 (extended summer and hols)
Compass Rose ($–$$)
Good
Moderate (additional charge for Fightertown Flight Simulators)

29E4

Merritt Island Refuge

- SR406 (4 miles E of Titusville)
- 321/861 0667
- Visitor Center, Mon–Fri 8–4:30, Sat–Sun 9–5. Closed Sun Feb–Oct

29F3

Elliott Museum

- 825 NE Ocean Boulevard/A1A
- 561/225 1961
- Daily 10–4
- Moderate

29D3

- 3708 Patten Avenue (US301 E), Ellenton
- 941/723 4536
- Daily 8–sunset; visitor center 8–4:30; tours Mon, Thu–Sun 9:30, 10:30, 1, 2, 3, 4
- Limited
- Cheap

29D4

- 4150 S Suncoast Boulevard/US19, Homosassa
- 352/628 5343
- Daily 9–5:30
- Concessions ($)
- Moderate

FLORIDA'S SPACE COAST

The big draw here is the terrific Kennedy Space Center (▶ 17). Within clear sight of the launch pad, the Space Coast can also offer the unspoiled dunes of the Canaveral National Seashore and the marshland wilderness area protected by **Merritt Island National Wildlife Refuge**. To the south, the 20-mile strip of barrier island beach between Cocoa Beach and Melbourne has been developed as a family resort.

FORT PIERCE ✪

Founded on the site of a Seminole War army outpost, Fort Pierce's main claims to fame are the barrier beaches of Hutchinson Island across the Indian River. A favorite spot for snorkeling is Bathtub Beach, and surfers congregate at Fort Pierce State Recreation Area or Pepper Beach. Down near Stuart Beach, the **Elliott Museum** makes an interesting stop. It is named after inventor Sterling Elliott and contains a variety of historic and eccentric exhibits.

GAMBLE PLANTATION ✪✪✪

The last remaining antebellum house in southern Florida, this gracious two-story mansion was built by sugar planter Major Robert Gamble in the 1840s. Two-foot thick walls and through breezes help keep the house cool in summer and the interior has been restored and furnished with period antiques. At the height of its productivity around 200 slaves worked Gamble's 3,500-acre plantation, and tours of the house include many interesting snippets of information about plantation life.

HOMOSASSA SPRINGS STATE WILDLIFE PARK

One of Florida's original natural tourist attractions, Homosassa Springs is a favorite manatee playground and showcase for several of the state's other endangered animal species. An underwater observatory in the 46ft-deep spring gives an unusual perspective on life in the Homosassa River, while pontoon boat rides are good for wildlife-spotting along the riverbank. Look for alligators, otters, and native birds. Florida black bears, bob cats, and deer can be seen in natural habitat enclosures.

JUNO BEACH MARINELIFE CENTER ✪
Each summer (Jun–Aug), Juno Beach is transformed into a major loggerhead sea turtle nesting ground (➤ 13). The excellent Marinelife Center has turtle tanks and a turtle nursery, natural history and marine displays, and organizes guided beach walks (reservations advised).

✚ 29F2
✉ 14200 US1, Juno Beach
☎ 561/627 8280
⊘ Tue–Sat 10–4, Sun 12–3
⬗ Cheap

JUPITER ✪
Once the northern terminus of the 1880s Lake Worth Railroad, which numbered Mars, Venus, and Juno among its stops, Jupiter's landmark red lighthouse is hard to miss. It's an offshoot of the Burt Reynolds' Ranch, a strange exercise in hagiography filled with memorabilia. More interesting is the **Florida History Center and Museum**, with collections of Native American and pioneer artifacts.

✚ 29F3

Florida History Center and Museum
✉ 805 N US1
☎ 561/747 6639
⊘ Tue–Fri 10–5, Sat–Sun 12–5
♿ Good
⬗ Cheap

> ### *Did you know ?*
>
> *Florida manatees (*Trichechus manatus*) are also called sea cows. They are vegetarians and generally grow to between nine and 12 feet, and weigh 1,000 to 2,500 pounds. Their sole enemy is man—but he is formidable enough—and there are only 1,500 to 2,500 manatees left in Florida waters.*

Facing page: *traditional Florida architecture*
Below: *feeding time for the manatees*

In the Know

If you only have a short time to visit Florida, or would like to get a real flavor of the state, here are some ideas:

10 Good Places to Have Lunch

Anthony's ($)
✉ 111 Duval Street, Key West ☎ 305/296 8899. Tasty Greek specialities and terrific salads.

Carmine's ($)
✉ 1802 E 7th Street, Ybor City (Tampa) ☎ 813/248 3834. Mountainous Cuban sandwiches.

Flakowitz Bagel Inn ($)
✉ 1999 N Federal Highway, Boca Raton ☎ 561/368 0666. Bagels stuffed to bursting point with all manner of goodies.

The Garden Restaurant ($)
✉ 217 Central Avenue, St Petersburg ☎ 727/896 3800. Lunchtime specials

10 Ways to Be a Local

Go fishing—freshwater lakes and streams, beaches, bridges, and fishing piers all offer excellent fishing.

Dress down for Florida, the locals are pretty much strangers to formal dress.

Go to a rodeo, one of the rare times Floridians do dress up—in cowboy gear.

Adopt a manatee—manatee rescue operations and refuges are always glad of a donation.

Say 'conk' not 'conch' like a true local (► 6).

Enjoy a margarita on the beach at sunset.

Tipping—do not betray your out-of-state origins by failing to tip.

Tuck into a dolphin—no, not Flipper, the warm-blooded mammal. Dolphin fish is a favorite on Florida seafood menus.

Turn right on red—unless signs say

Above: *overhead traffic lights are a common sight*

otherwise, drivers in Florida can turn right on a red light (as long as the way is clear, of course).

Send back the Key lime pie if it is green, true Key limes are yellow.

include *meze* and pasta.

The Hut Restaurant and Tiki Bar ($)

✉ John's Pass Boardwalk, Madiera Beach ☎ 727/393 7749. Alfresco dining in this recreation of a fishing village.

Lombard's Landing ($$)

✉ Universal Studios, Orlando ☎ 407/224 6400. One of Orlando's best theme park restaurants.

Mark's at the Park ($)

✉ Mizner Park, Boca Raton ☎ 561/395 0770. Great menu and alfresco dining.

The Monk's Vineyard ($$)

✉ 56 St George Street, St Augustine ☎ 904/824 5888. Pretty terrace setting for good pub grub.

News Café ($–$$)

✉ 800 Ocean Drive, Miami Beach ☎ 305/538 6397. Omelettes, salads and pasta, with sea view.

Palm Pavilion Beachside Grill ($$$)

✉ 18 Bay Esplanade, Clearwater Beach ☎ 727/446 4626. The Palm Pavilion's outside deck allows casual dining.

10

Top Activities

Birdwatching: Corkscrew Swamp Sanctuary (➤ 41), Merritt Island National Wildlife Refuge (➤ 54), and the Florida Keys are among the top spots.

Boat trips: notable boating areas include the Lee Island Coast (➤ 24), the Everglades (➤ 41), and the Keys (➤ 46).

Canoeing: many riverfront state parks provide canoe trails (➤ 110).

Diving: coral reef diving in the Keys (➤ 46) and fascinating wreck sites off the Emerald Coast (➤ 76, 77).

Fishing: licenses are required. Check at bait and tackle shops (➤ 111).

Golf: Florida is one of the world's top golfing destinations with over 1,000 golf courses around the state (➤ 112).

Motorsports: major events at Daytona International Speedway (➤ 74), and Homestead-Miami Speedway (➤ 113).

Polo: a top winter pursuit on the Gold Coast (➤ 113).

Tennis: numerous hotel and public courts (➤ 112).

Watersports: hotels and beachfront concessions rent out windsurfing, sailing, kayaking, and dive equipment (➤ 112).

10

Top Beaches

- Bahia Honda State Recreation Area (➤ 47)
- Caladesi Island State Park (➤ 63)
- Daytona Beach (➤ 74–5)
- Grayton Beach State Recreation Area (➤ 78)
- Kathryn Abbey Hanna State Park (➤ 81)
- Miami Beach (➤ 35)
- Red Reef Park, Boca Raton (➤ 40)
- St Andrews State Recreation Area (➤ 85)
- Sanibel and Captiva Islands (➤ 24)
- Siesta Key, Sarasota (➤ 25)

Below and left: *sunglasses and minimal clothing are the order of the day in Florida*

29E3

Fast food, cafés/ restaurants ($–$$)

A World of Orchids

2501 N Old Lake Wilson Road (CR545)

407/396 1887

Tue–Sun 9:30–4:30

Good

Moderate

Gatorland

14501 S Orange Blossom Trail/US441

407/855 5496 or 1-800 393 5297

Daily 9–dusk

Good

Expensive

limited

Moderate

The gaping entrance to Gatorland

KENNEDY SPACE CENTER (▶ 17, TOP TEN)

KISSIMMEE ✪

A budget dormitory annexe for Walt Disney World to the south of Orlando, Kissimmee stretches for more than 20 miles along US192 in a seamless strip of hotels, motels, shopping malls, and family restaurants. To help visitors find their way around, Navigational Markers (NM) have been posted along the route.

Along the main road (US192), family-style attractions range from miniature golf and fairground rides outside the Old Town Kissimmee shopping mall (▶ 105) to dinner theaters. A World of Orchids (12 miles west) has a half-acre conservatory housing thousands of orchids and hundreds of tropical plants, including bromeliads and ferns, alongside chameleons and birds. If you'd prefer to study native Floridian flora and fauna, then take to the water on Boggy Creek Airboat Rides. The half hour rides offer close-up encounters with alligators, water birds, and turtles.

Just north of Kissimmee, visitors receive a snappy welcome from a pair of outsize alligator jaws at Gatorland. This old-fashioned but enduringly popular attraction features hundreds of alligators, 'gator-wrestling shows, educational presentations, an assortment of turtles and snakes, and a boardwalk trail through a marshland alligator breeding ground and bird preserve.

Thoroughbred horses graze Ocala's rich pastures

MOUNT DORA ✪

A pretty lakeside country town set in the citrus groves north of Orlando, Mount Dora was founded back in the 1870s. The restored downtown district offers an attractive selection of gift shops, galleries, and cafés, there are boat trips and walks around the lake, and the Chamber of Commerce distributes drive tour maps to the town's historic Victorian homes.

🔢 29E4
🍴 Windsor Rose English Tea Room ($–$$), 144 W 4th Avenue ☎ 352/735 2551
❓ Drive tour maps from Chamber of Commerce, 341 Alexander Street

OCALA ✪✪

The rolling pastures of Marion County are the center of Florida's billion-dollar horse-breeding industry, bordering the vast pinewood preserve of the Ocala National Forest. Ten miles east of Ocala, the 400,000-acre national forest offers a range of outdoor activities including excellent hiking trails, fishing, boating, swimming, and some of the most attractive canoe trails in the state (➤ 110).

On the edge of the forest, glass-bottomed boat rides at **Silver Springs** have been a local sightseeing feature since 1878. The world's largest artesian spring is now part of a theme park attraction with Silver River cruises, exotic animals, and Jeep safaris touring the woodlands where the original Tarzan movies were filmed in the 1930s.

🔢 29D4
❓ Details of horse farm visits: Ocala Chamber of Commerce, 110 E Silver Springs Boulevard ☎ 352/629 8051

Silver Springs
✉ 5656 E Silver Springs Boulevard
☎ 352/236 2121
🕐 Daily 10–5 (extended summer and hols)
♿ Limited
💷 Very expensive

ORLANDO ✪✪✪

Launched into the limelight by the opening of Disney's Magic Kingdom in 1971, Orlando is the undisputed world capital of theme parks and a bustling modern city 15 miles north of the Walt Disney World Resort (➤ 70–71). The main tourist area is in the south around International Drive, or I-Drive as it is generally known. It runs parallel to the I-4 highway, which helps cut journey times between the city's widely spread attractions.

The biggest attraction on (or just off) I-Drive is **Universal Orlando,** with its two theme parks and the CityWalk shopping, dining, and entertainment district. Universal Studio's top rides include Back to the Future and the interactive MEN IN BLACK Alien Attack, the world's first life-size, ride-through video game. Don't miss the excellent Terminator 2: 3-D show and things get pretty wild in the hurricane zone at Twister.

🔢 29E4
🍴 Fast food, cafés, restaurants ($–$$$)
🚌 I-Ride service along International Drive between Belz Factory Mall and SeaWorld

Universal Orlando
🔢 60B2
✉ 1000 Universal Studios Plaza
☎ 407/363 8000 or 1-888 837 2273
🕐 Daily
♿ Very good
💷 Very expensive

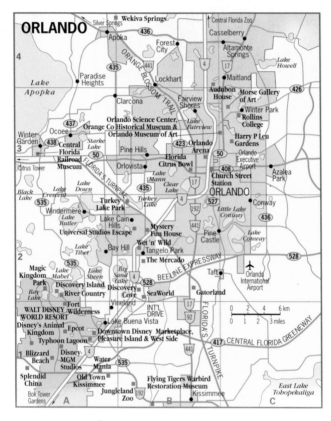

ORLANDO

SeaWorld Orlando

- 60B2
- 7007 SeaWorld Drive
- 407/351 3600 or 1-800 327 2424
- Daily 9–7 (extended summer and hols)
- Concessions, cafés and family restaurants ($–$$$)
- I-Ride, Lynx 42
- Very good
- Very expensive

Universal's second park, Islands of Adventure, is a homage to the comicstrip. Guests receive a ticket to ride the cartoons from the heights of the Incredible Hulk Roller Coaster and Doctor Doom's Fearfall to the depths of Popeye and Bluto's Bilge-Rat Barges raft ride. The world's most technologically advanced theme park (allegedly) is also the place to get to grips with the fantastic robotic models of Jurassic Park, the fantasy world of the Lost Continent, and the whimsical Seuss Landing.

Heading south of I-Drive, SeaWorld is Orlando's other major theme park. The world's most popular marine park offers a full day of entertaining shows starring killer whales, dolphins, sea lions, and more. In between the shows, there are fantastic aquarium displays, the

Discovery Cove
- 60B2
- 6000 Discovery Cove Way
- 407/370 1280 or 1-800 327 2424
- Daily (check schedules)
- Very expensive

Orlando Science Center
- 60B/C3
- 777 E Princeton Street
- 407/514 2000 or 1-800 672 4386
- Mon–Thu 9–5, Fri–Sat 9–9, Sun 12–5
- Very good
- Moderate

Harry P. Leu Gardens
- 60C3
- 1920 N Forest Avenue
- 407/246 2620
- Daily 9–5
- Good
- Moderate
- Leu House tours, daily every 30 mins

enchanting Penguin Encounter, manatees, touch tanks, polar bears, and beluga whales as well as the Kraken roller coaster and Journey To Atlantis thrill ride. SeaWorld's sister park, **Discovery Cove**, specialises in interactive marine adventures. Park admission is restricted to 1,000 visitors a day and the lucky few can experience a raft of water-based activities including snorkeling in the Coral Reef pool and swimming with bottlenose dolphins.

Downtown Orlando rises in a miniature forest of mirrored glass towers on the shores of Lake Eola. Wonderworks on I-Drive offers interactive games, concentrating on fun science exhibits. Hard Rock Vault, also on I-Drive, is Hard Rock's first "museum" with thousands of items of genuine rock memorabilia. The area has also attracted a wide choice of restaurants and bars.

To the north, the terrific **Orlando Science Center** is one of the best science museums in the state. Laid out on four levels beneath a landmark silver observatory dome, the museum is packed with dozens of eye-catching and entertaining interactive exhibits, Florida habitat displays, movie special effects demonstrations and a planetarium.

Nearby, the gorgeous **Harry P. Leu Gardens** offer gentle strolls on the banks of Lake Rowena and impressive formal rose gardens. In springtime the magnolias burst into color with a spectacular show of camellias planted by the Leus, who lived at the heart of the gardens. Their much enlarged pioneer home is open for tours.

The pretty northeastern suburb of Winter Park also makes a delightful escape from the crowds. There is upscale shopping on Park Avenue, boat trips on Lake Osceola, and a superb collection of Tiffany glassware and art nouveau at the Morse Gallery of Art.

North of Orlando

Distance
120 miles (plus 20 for the detour)

Time
8 hours with stops

Start/end point
Orlando
🛡 29E4

Lunch
Take a picnic to Ocala National Forest. Concession stand ($) only at Juniper Springs

This day trip covers three diverse central Florida sights.

From Orlando, take SR50 west to Clermont (22 miles), then north on US27 to Lakeridge Winery and Vineyards (6 miles).

Surrounded by fields striped with rows of vines, a Visitor Center offers guided tours of the winery followed by free tastings of red, white, and sparkling wines.

Continue north on US27 to SR19 N (3 miles). Follow SR19 north all the way to the Ocala National Forest (30 miles). The southern Visitor Center is just inside the forest on the left.

Drop in at the Visitor Center to pick up maps and brochures giving details of the national forest's numerous outdoor attractions (► 59). One of the nicest spots is the Juniper Springs Recreation Area.

An enticing array of shops line Mount Dora's quiet streets

To reach Juniper Springs, keep north on SR19 to SR40, then turn left (west). The entrance is on the right. Take SR19 south for a direct route to Mount Dora. For a more scenic detour, keep west on SR40 to CR314-A, turn left and follow the forest road south. Two miles beyond CR464, turn right onto SE 182nd Av Road (by a corner store). At CR42 (7½ miles) turn left, then right (1 mile) still on CR42 for Eustis (11 miles), and pick up signs for Mount Dora (9 miles).

Renowned for its genteel Victorian architecture, speciality shopping, and tempting tea shops, Mount Dora is a charming place to stop for a break (► 59).

Take 5th Avenue to Old 441 South, which joins US441 (3 miles), the road back to Orlando (20 miles).

PINELLAS SUNCOAST ✪✪

A 28-mile strip of hotel-lined barrier island beaches, the Pinellas Suncoast is the busiest resort area on the Gulf coast. The two liveliest districts are St. Pete Beach in the south, and Clearwater Beach in the north, both of which make good seaside bases for trips around the Tampa Bay area. From Clearwater Beach, there are boat services to gorgeous Caladesi Island, a barrier island preserve with one of the finest beaches in the country.

The area has a couple of low-key attractions, the best of which is the **Pinellas County Heritage Village**, a collection of 28 carefully restored historic buildings. Pioneer cabins, Edwardian homes, a church, and a train station are among the exhibits. Another popular stop is the Suncoast Seabird Sanctuary, which rescues and rehabilitates pelicans, herons, egrets, and other birds.

➕ 66A3
🍴 Cafés/restaurants ($–$$$)
🔄 St. Petersburg (➤ 23), Sarasota (➤ 25), Tampa (➤ below)

Pinellas County Heritage Village
✉ 11909 125th Street N, Largo
☎ 727/582 2123
🕐 Tue–Sat 10–4, Sun 1–4
♿ Good
🎫 Free (donations welcome)

ST. PETERSBURG (➤ 23, TOP TEN)

SARASOTA (➤ 25, TOP TEN)

TAMPA ✪✪✪

A hopping bayfront city, Tampa boasts some of the most varied and exciting attractions on the Gulf coast. Henry Plant brought the railroad to town in 1884 and built a grand hotel to house the expected flood of tourists. The city's prospects improved further with the arrival of Cuban cigar workers in 1886, who established themselves at Ybor City. Plant's lavish Moorish Revival-style hotel is a local landmark. Its silver onion-domed minarets act as a beacon for visitors crossing the Hillsborough River from downtown to look around the **Henry B. Plant Museum** housed in a suite of former hotel rooms.

Pelicans ready for lunch at Suncoast Seabird Sanctuary

➕ 29D3
🍴 Cafés/restaurants ($–$$$)
🔄 Lowry Park Zoo (➤ 109), St. Petersburg (➤ 23)

Henry B Plant Museum
✉ 401 W JF Kennedy Boulevard
☎ 813/254 1891
🕐 Tue–Sat 10–4, Sun 12–4
♿ Good
🎫 Donations

63

Tampa Museum of Art
- ✉ 600 N Ashley Drive
- ☎ 813/274 8130
- ⏰ Tue–Sat 10–5 (3rd Thu of month 10–8), Sun 11–5
- ♿ Very good
- 🎟 Cheap

Florida Aquarium
- ✉ 701 Channelside Drive
- ☎ 813/273 4021
- ⏰ Daily 9:30–5
- ♿ Very good
- 🎟 Expensive

Busch Gardens
- ✉ 3000 E Busch Boulevard (at 40th Street)
- ☎ 813/987 5082
- ⏰ Daily 9:30–6 (extended summer and hols)
- ♿ Good
- 🎟 Very expensive

Museum of Science and Industry (MOSI)
- ✉ 4801 E Fowler Avenue
- ☎ 813/987 6100
- ⏰ Mon–Thu 9–5, Sat and Sun 9–7
- ♿ Very good
- 🎟 Expensive

Downtown Tampa is compact and easy to explore on foot. Backing onto the river, the **Tampa Museum of Art** displays fine collections of Greek and Roman antiquities and 20th-century American art, shown in rotation, and hosts interesting traveling exhibitions.

Down on the waterfront, the terrific **Florida Aquarium** should not be missed. Displays follow a drop of water from the Florida aquifer on its journey to the sea via river and swamp dioramas inhabited by live waterbirds, otters, and freshwater fish. There are scurrying crabs in Bays and Beaches, a Coral Reef exhibit with dive demonstrations, and Offshore tanks showcasing local marine life.

Out to the east of the city, Tampa's top crowd-puller is the huge African-inspired **Busch Gardens** theme park, which doubles as one of the nation's premier zoos. More than 3,300 animals roam the central 160-acre Serengeti Plain and appear in special exhibits such as the Great Ape Domain and the Edge of Africa safari experience. Busch Gardens is also famous for its thrill rides including Montu, one of the world's tallest and longest inverted roller coasters, and the spectacular Tanganyika Tidal Wave.

Just down the road from Busch Gardens, the **Museum of Science and Industry** (generally referred to as MOSI) inhabits a striking modern architectural complex. Here, imaginative interactive displays tackle the mysteries of the world about us and the GTE Challenger Learning Center turns the spotlight on to space travel and research.

Roller coaster fans experience Montu, the top thrill ride at Busch Gardens

A Walk Around Ybor City

Tampa's historic cigar-making quarter has undergone a modest renaissance. Old cigar factories and workers' cottages now house shops, cafés, and restaurants, and the weekend club scene is hugely popular. The starting point is Ybor Square, the original red-brick cigar factory, which has been transformed into a shopping mall.

Turn left out of the front entrance onto Avenida Republica de Cuba for a short walk to the corner of 9th Avenue.

On the opposite corner are the arcades of the old Cherokee Club, once patronized by Cuban freedom fighter José Martí, Teddy Roosevelt and Winston Churchill.

Turn right for one block on 9th, leading directly to the Ybor City State Museum. It is more fun to walk down 15th Street and along 7th Avenue, or La Septima, Ybor City's main shopping street. Cut back up to 9th Avenue at 18th Street; turn right.

The museum tells the story of the cigar industry and the migrants who came to work here. Down the street, a worker's "shotgun" cottage has been restored.

Cut across the plaza by the Immigrant Statue to 19th Street. Rejoin 7th Avenue, and turn left.

The walk-in humidor at Columbia Restaurant Cigar Store, number 2014, is one of several interesting stops along this section of La Septima. The Columbia Restaurant building, on the corner of 21st Street, is lavishly adorned with hand-painted tiles.

Walk back down 7th Avenue with its fashion stores, design emporiums, and gift shops.

Distance
1½ miles

Time
2 hours with stops

Start/end point
Ybor Square
🚇 67E4
🚌 8, 46

Lunch
Little Sicily ($)
✉ 1724 8th Avenue E (at 18th Street)
☎ 813/248 2940

Did you know ?
The name Tampa means 'sticks of fire', and around 500 million cigars are produced in the city each year. Annual sales are in the region of $150 million.

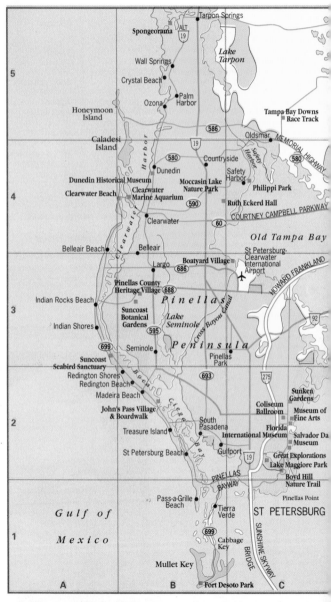

Tarpon Springs

Spongeorama

Lake Tarpon

Wall Springs

Crystal Beach

Ozona • Palm Harbor

Honeymoon Island

Tampa Bay Downs Race Track

Oldsmar

MEMORIAL HIGHWAY

Caladesi Island

Countryside

Safety Harbor

Dunedin

Dunedin Historical Museum

Clearwater Beach

Clearwater Marine Aquarium

Moccasin Lake Nature Park

Philippi Park

Ruth Eckerd Hall

COURTNEY CAMPBELL PARKWAY

Clearwater

Old Tampa Bay

Belleair Beach

Belleair

St Petersburg-Clearwater International Airport

Largo

Boatyard Village

HOWARD FRANKLAND

Pinellas County Heritage Village

Pinellas

Indian Rocks Beach

Suncoast Botanical Gardens

Lake Seminole

Indian Shores

Peninsula

Seminole

Pinellas Park

Suncoast Seabird Sanctuary

Redington Shores

Redington Beach

Madeira Beach

John's Pass Village & Boardwalk

South Pasadena

Sunken Gardens

Coliseum Ballroom

Museum of Fine Arts

Florida International Museum

Salvador Dali Museum

Treasure Island

St Petersburg Beach

Gulfport

Great Explorations

Lake Maggiore Park

Boyd Hill Nature Trail

Pinellas Point

PINELLAS BAYWAY

ST PETERSBURG

Gulf of Mexico

Pass-a-Grille Beach

Tierra Verde

Cabbage Key

Mullet Key

Fort Desoto Park

SUNSHINE SKYWAY BRIDGE

A   B   C

1   2   3   4   5

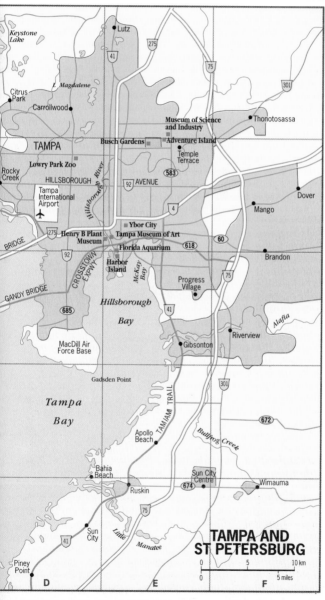

Keystone
Lake

Lutz

275

41

75

301

Citrus
Park

L. Magdalene

Carrollwood

Thonotosassa

**Museum of Science
and Industry**

TAMPA

■ **Busch Gardens** ■ **Adventure Island**

Rocky
Creek

Lowry Park Zoo

Temple
Terrace

HILLSBOROUGH

583

Hillsborough River

92 AVENUE

4

Tampa
International
Airport

Dover

Mango

275

BRIDGE

**Henry B Plant
Museum**

■ **Ybor City**

Tampa Museum of Art

60

618

92

Florida Aquarium

**Harbor
Island**

Brandon

CROSSTOWN EXPWY

McKay
Bay

GANDY BRIDGE

685

**Hillsborough
Bay**

Progress
Village

75

41

Alafia

**MacDill Air
Force Base**

Riverview

Gibsonton

Gadsden Point

301

Tampa

672

Bay

Apollo
Beach

TAMIAMI TRAIL

Bullfrog Creek

Bahia
Beach

Sun City
Centre

Wimauma

Ruskin

674

75

41

Sun
City

Little

Manatee

**TAMPA AND
ST PETERSBURG**

Piney
Point

0   5   10 km

0   5 miles

D   E   F

67

Around Tampa Bay

Distance
125 miles

Time
8 hours including stops

Start/end point
St Petersburg
66C2

Lunch
Banyan Café ($)
Ringling Museum of Art
941/359 3181

*The Sunshine Skyway
Bridge spans Tampa Bay*

The start point for this day trip around Tampa Bay is downtown St. Petersburg.

> *Take 4th Street/US92 north and east across Gandy Bridge to connect with the Tampa's Crosstown Expressway. The Florida Aquarium exit is 6B.*

The $84-million state-of-the-art Florida Aquarium makes a fascinating interlude (► 64).

> *Rejoin the Expressway heading east (direction Brandon), to Exit 15–A. Take I-75 south (direction Naples) to Exit 43 (30 miles). Turn onto US301 south for 1 mile to Ellenton for the Gamble Plantation.*

The historic Gamble mansion is a fine example of mid-19th-century antebellum architecture (► 54).

> *Rejoin I-75 south to Exit 40 (12 miles), and follow University Parkway right to the gates of the Ringling Museum (7 miles) in Sarasota.*

Circus king John Ringling's magnificent winter home and estate overlook Sarasota Bay (► 25).

> *From the Ringling Museum of Art, US41 heads north to connect with US19, the direct route to the Sunshine Skyway bridge and St. Petersburg (40 miles). If you have time for a swim, turn south on US41. Continue for 3 miles, bear right for St. Armands Key (SR789 N), and cross the John Ringling Causeway. Keep right following SR789 N along the barrier island beaches.*

A recommended place to stop here is Bradenton Beach, which has an attractive strip of cafés, stores, and water-sports concessions facing the Gulf.

> *SR64 leads back to US41 at Bradenton.*

The 4-mile Sunshine Skyway is quite an attraction in its own right. Dedicated in 1987, it has a record 1,200ft main span rising 175ft above the entrance to Tampa Bay.

TARPON SPRINGS ✪

A little piece of Florida that is forever Greek, the sponge fishing center of Tarpon Springs has a distinctly Mediterranean air. Greek divers first came here to harvest the Gulf sponge beds in the early 1900s. As well as their sponging skills they imported a hefty slice of Greek culture, which has turned the dockside town into something of a tourist magnet.

Piles of sponges decorate Dodecanese Boulevard, the bustling main thoroughfare, where sidewalk cafés play bouzouki music and sell ouzo. Join one of the narrated boat trips around the docks for a lesson in local history, and drop in on the **Tarpon Springs Aquarium** for a peek at the local marine life. For scrumptious treats, be sure to sample the delicious Greek pastries on sale in a host of bakeries.

Natural sponges for sale at Tarpon Springs

🔲 66B5
🍴 Cafés/restaurants ($–$$$)

Tarpon Springs Aquarium
✉ 850 Dodecanese Boulevard
☎ 727/938 5378
🕐 Mon–Sat 10–5, Sun 12–5
♿ Good
🎟 Cheap

VERO BEACH ✪

Chosen by Disney for their first Florida seaside resort, Vero Beach has a reputation for charming vacation homes, a celebrated arts center, and muted luxury. Galleries and boutiques gather on Ocean Drive, near the landmark Driftwood Resort. This eccentric oceanfront property was founded in the 1930s, and is partially constructed from driftwood washed ashore on the beach.

North of town, along the Treasure Coast, the **Sebastian Inlet State Recreation Area** is a favorite with surfers and fishermen. The McLarty Treasure Museum describes how the Treasure Coast got its name when the Spanish Plate Fleet was dashed onto the reefs during a storm in 1715.

🔲 29F3
🍴 Cafés/restaurants ($–$$$)

Sebastian Inlet State Recreation Area
✉ 9700 S A1A
☎ 321/984 4852
🕐 Daily 8–dusk, museum 10–5
♿ Good 🎟 Cheap

The Driftwood Inn at Vero Beach

+ 60A1

✉ Lake Buena Vista (20 miles south of Orlando)

☎ Information: 407/939 4636; reservations: 407/934 7639

🕐 Check current schedules

🍴 Each park offers a choice throughout the day. Make reservations at Guest Relations for table service restaurants ($$–$$$)

🚌 Free bus from many Orlando/Kissimmee hotels. Walt Disney World transportation operates from the Magic Kingdom ticketing center

♿ Excellent

💜 Very expensive

❓ Details of daily parades, shows, fireworks and laser displays are in park guides

Above: *geting close to the wildlife in Disney's Animal Kingdom*

Fastpass
Beat the lines with the time-saving Disney FASTPASS designed to cut waiting times on the most popular rides in all four parks. Insert your admission ticket into the FASTPASS machines at the rides offering the complimentary service and you'll receive a designated ride time.

WALT DISNEY WORLD RESORT ✪✪✪

Walt Disney World (➤ 26) is truly a world within a world. The biggest entertainment complex on the planet boasts four theme parks, two water parks, and enough shopping, dining, and nightlife to keep the family entertained full time. Around 23 million guests visit Walt Disney World annually, and it can get extremely busy. Avoid vacation periods if you can; the most comfortable times to visit, both on the crowd and the weather front, are mid-September until mid-December, and January until mid-February. The Disney experience does not come cheap, but tickets (➤ panel opposite) can be purchased ahead, which helps with budget planning as well as cutting down on lining up at the gates; reservations for accommodations should be made well in advance.

The following is a *very* brief guide to the best that Walt Disney World has to offer.

Disney's Animal Kingdom The largest of the Disney theme parks (five times bigger than the Magic Kingdom) opened in the spring of 1998. The giant 14-story Tree of Life towers over Discovery Island at the heart of the park, linked by bridges to Africa, Asia, DinoLand U.S.A., and the small child-friendly Camp Minnie-Mickey. Top rides include Kilimanjaro Safaris into the 100-acre African savannah for close encounters with exotic animals and in DinoLand U.S.A. the dramatic DINOSAUR! adventure.

Disney-MGM Studios A fun Hollywood-style setting for rides and shows culled from Disney's favorite movies. The Disney-MGM Backlot Tour and The Magic of Disney animation step behind the scenes of the studio, while live shows draw inspiration from blockbuster successes such as *The Voyage of the Little Mermaid* and *Beauty and the Beast*. The best thrill rides are Twilight Zone™ Tower of Terror and the Rock 'n' Roller Starring Aerosmith.

Downtown Disney Marketplace, Pleasure Island and West Side A mega entertainment district on the shores of Lake Buena Vista, Downtown Disney encompasses shopping, celebrity restaurants, and entertainments. The new Disney West Side attractions include a giant movie theater complex and theater, while the Pleasure Island nightlife zone has no fewer than eight clubs, which run the gamut from 1970s disco hits to country music.

Epcot A park in two parts, Disney's Experimental Prototype Community of Tomorrow looks at the world about us. Future World tackles things scientific with typical Disney flair. Highlights include The Living Seas aquarium, the boat ride through experimental gardens in The Land, the fantastic dinosaur romp in Universe of Energy and Spaceship Earth. World Showcase presents 11 pavilions, set around the Lagoon, depicting the potted architecture and culture of nations as diverse as Canada and China.

MAGIC KINGDOM (➤ 26, TOP TEN)

Water Parks Disney's two water parks are enormously popular for a day away from the theme park trail. The biggest and arguably the best is Blizzard Beach with its bizarre ski resort theme and mountainous water slides including the dramatic 60mph Summit Plummet slide. Typhoon Lagoon goes for the shipwrecked tropical look, a huge wave-pool lagoon and rafting adventures.

WEEKI WACHEE SPRINGS WATERPARK ✪
One of those truly weird "only in Florida" attractions, this veteran theme park's unique selling point is its underwater ballets performed by live "mermaids." For students of the kitsch it is a must. Less unusual attractions include a wilderness river cruise, a water park with waterslides, riverfront picnic area, and sandy beach.

Ticket Options

For short-stay visitors, the only ticket option available is one-day one-park tickets. For longer stay visitors, and those planning to return either later on the vacation or years hence, 5 and 7 Day Park Hopper Plus Passes offer unbeatable flexibility, plus savings on single day tickets. The Passes cover unlimited admission to all four theme parks and a choice of entries to the water parks, Pleasure Island and Disney's Wide World of Sport. Pass-holders are free to hop from park to park on the same day and use the transportation system, and unused days never expire.

Above: *Epcot's trademark, the silver Spaceship Earth geosphere, is a time machine in which you ride from the past to the stars*

🔲 29D4
✉ US19 at SR 50
☎ 352/596 2062 or 1-800 678 9335
🕐 Daily 9:30–5:30
🍴 Mermaid Gallery (£)
👋 Moderate

71

Northern Florida

Northern Florida is the cradle of the state, where 16th-century Spanish explorers, pioneer adventurers and plantation owners put down roots long before the advent of the railroad. Bordered by Georgia and Alabama, the north has a distinctly Old South feel, particularly in the Panhandle, where attitudes are more old-fashioned and antebellum architecture nestles beneath giant live oaks.

Between Pensacola and the fishing villages and marshlands of the Big Bend, the Panhandle's blinding quartz sand beaches are the most spectacular in the state. Inland are glassy clear streams and rivers, such as the famous Suwannee.

The other face of the north is the First Coast, which unfurls along the Atlantic shore between the strikingly dissimilar resorts of cosy Fernandina Beach, historic St. Augustine, and bold-as-brass Daytona—all easily reached from Orlando.

"Way down upon de Swanee ribber, Far, far away, Dere's wha' my heart is turning ebber, Dere's wha' de old folks stay."

STEPHEN C FOSTER
Old Folks at Home (1851)

———————•———————

A Daytona lifeguard mans his beach station

What to See in Northern Florida

APALACHICOLA

28C5
Cafés/restaurants ($–$$$)
Walking tour maps available from the Chamber of Commerce, 99 Market Street, Suite 100. Florida Seafood Festival, first weekend in Nov

Florida's premier oyster producer, this delightful small town lies at the mouth of the Apalachicola River, which feeds the nutrient-rich oyster beds in the bay. Down by the docks, the old brick cotton warehouses stand testament to Apalachicola's days as a thriving 19th-century customs post, and around town there are dozens of gracious old homes built by successful merchants. There is no beach, but St. George Island has a beautiful strip of barrier island shore across the causeway from Eastpoint.

CEDAR KEY

29D4
Cafés/restaurants ($–$$)

Manatee Springs State Park
SR320 (6 miles W of Chiefland)
352/493 6072
Daily 8–dusk
Cheap

At the southern extent of the Big Bend, where the Panhandle meets the Florida peninsula, this quirky and weatherbeaten fishing village looks out over the Gulf of Mexico from the tail end of a string of tiny island keys. It is a laid-back retreat for fishermen and birdwatchers with boat trips, seafood restaurants, and a funny little museum telling the story of the 19th-century logging boom that cleared the namesake cedar forests.

This is also a good base for trips to **Manatee Springs State Park**, a favorite wintering spot for manatees, with hiking paths and canoe trails on the Suwannee River.

DAYTONA

29E4
Cafés/restaurants ($–$$$)
Speedweeks/Daytona 500, Feb; Bike Week, Mar; Biketoberfest, Oct

DAYTONA USA
1801 W International Speedway Boulevard
386/947 6800
Daily 9–6
Very good
Expensive

Daytona's love affair with the combustion engine dates back to the early 1900s, when the likes of Henry Ford, Louis Chevrolet, and Harvey Firestone flocked south to enjoy the winter sunshine. Today, the "World Center of Racing" divides its attractions between the hotel-lined sands of Daytona Beach and mainland Daytona across the Halifax River.

Daytona Beach's chief attraction is the broad sandy shore, which is fully geared up for watersports and old-time family fun. There are amusement arcades, fishing, dining, and aerial gondola rides on Ocean Pier, cotton candy and go-karts on The Boardwalk, and an open-air bandshell. A rather bizarre selling

Daytona International Speedway is a must for racing fans

point is that you can drive along the beach for a small fee, though speeds are nothing like those of the racers that broke the world land speed record here during the pioneer days of car racing.

On the mainland, the biggest crowd-puller is Daytona International Speedway, home of the Daytona 500 and a state-of-the-art visitor center, **DAYTONA USA**. This is speed heaven with a range of interactive racing-themed exhibits, loads of memorabilia, a behind-the- scenes racing movie, and track tours on non-race days.

The **Museum of Arts and Sciences** has something for everyone. Children love the 130,000-year-old giant sloth skeleton and "hands-on" artifacts; there is also a superb collection of fine and decorative American arts and crafts in the Dow Gallery, plus a notable Cuban Museum, spotlighting Latin American culture from 1759 to 1959.

South of Daytona Beach, the **Ponce Inlet Lighthouse Museum** is a popular outing. Built in 1887, the 175ft tower affords far-reaching views along the coast. Down below, the old keeper's quarters display historical and nautical exhibits, and a special building houses a superb 17ft-tall first order Fresnel lens, which resembles an enormous glass and brass pine cone.

Museum of Arts and Sciences
✉ 1040 Museum Boulevard
☎ 386/255 0285
🕐 Tue–Fri 9–4, Sat–Sun 12–5
💲 Cheap

Ponce Inlet Lighthouse Museum
✉ 4931 S Peninsula Drive
☎ 386/761 1821
🕐 Daily 10–5
💲 Cheap

Did you know ?

Alexander Winton set the first land speed record on Daytona Beach in 1903. He was clocked at 68mph. Thirty-two years later Malcolm Campbell reached 276mph while setting the last world speed record to be established on the beach.

🕂 28B5

🍴 Cafés/restaurants ($–$$)

❓ Destin Fishing Rodeo and Seafood Festival, Oct

Above: *each building has a unique charm in Fernandina Beach*

🕂 28B5

✉ SR395, Port Washington

☎ 850/231 4214

🕐 Gardens, daily 8–dusk; house, guided tours Thu–Mon 9–4

💲 Gardens, free; house, cheap; parking, cheap

🕂 29E5

🍴 Cafés/restaurants ($–$$$)

❓ Historic district walking tours from Amelia Island Museum of History (opposite)

DESTIN ✪

Destin revels in the title of the "World's Luckiest Fishing Village." At the eastern end of the Emerald Coast, where the Gulf waters are indeed an incredible green, local marinas harbor the largest fleet of charter fishing boats in Florida, and trophy catches include blue marlin, tarpon, and wahoo. If putting out to sea in boats is not your thing, there is still the opportunity to impress—sizeable tarpon have been hooked off the 1,200ft Okaloosa Pier.

EDEN STATE GARDENS AND MANSION ✪✪

This charming antebellum-style mansion was built on the banks of the Choctawhatchee River by logging baron William H. Wesley in 1897. The house has been meticulously restored and furnished with antiques. Outside, shaded by towering southern magnolias and live oaks draped with Spanish moss, the lush lawn leads down to the water, where picnickers are welcome on the riverbank. One of the best times to visit is in spring, when the azaleas and camellias are in flower.

FERNANDINA BEACH ✪✪✪

At the northern corner of Amelia Island, facing Georgia across the St. Mary's River, Fernandina is a charming small resort and fishing centre famous for its 50-block Victorian Historic District.

At the heart of town, Center Street leads down to the wharves, where the shrimping fleet docks. Quiet streets are lined with a veritable lexicon of Victorian architectural

Amelia Island Museum of History
* 233 S 3rd Street
* 904/261 7378
* Mon–Sat 10–4, tours at 11 and 2
* Good
* Cheap

Fort Clinch State Park
* 2601 Atlantic Avenue
* 904/277 7274
* Daily 8–dusk
* Cheap

styles from Queen Anne homes and Italianate villas to ornate Chinese Chippendale creations built by logging barons and sea captains. Many of these are now bed-and-breakfast inns, and there are several luxurious resorts on the island.

Fernandina's checkered past is unraveled in the **Amelia Island Museum of History**. This strategic site has been fought over so many times it is known as the Isle of Eight Flags, and oral history tours of the museum are illustrated with centuries-old Timucua Indian artifacts and Spanish colonial relics. There is more history in store at **Fort Clinch State Park** where rangers adopt Civil War uniforms and take part in monthly historic re-enactments. In the grounds surrounding the massive 19th-century brick fort there are hiking trails, beaches, and a campsite.

Below: *sea lion shows are popular with visitors*

FORT WALTON ✪

The western anchor of the Emerald Coast, which stretches east in a 24-mile swathe of dazzling quartz sand to Destin (► 76), Fort Walton is a well-developed family resort with affordable accommodations, very safe swimming, watersports, fishing, and golf. As well as the glories of the beach, there is marine life entertainment at the **Gulfarium**. Regular dolphin and sea lion shows are interspersed by aquarium displays, the Living Sea exhibit with its sharks and sea turtles, free-ranging exotic birds, and enclosures for alligators and 600-pound gray seals.

North of the town, across Choctawhatchee Bay, the enormous Eglin Air Force Base welcomes visitors to the **U.S. Air Force Armament Museum**, the only museum in the U.S. dedicated to Air Force weaponry. Top exhibits include an SR-71 "Blackbird" spy plane. The Theater holds regular film show, *Arming the Air Force*, relating the history of the base which controls a 86,500-square mile flight test area above the Gulf of Mexico.

* 28B5
* Cafés/restaurants ($–$$$)

Gulfarium
* 1010 Miracle Strip Parkway/US98 E
* 850/243 9046
* Daily, Jun–Aug 9–8, Sep–May 9–6
* Expensive

U.S. Air Force Armament Museum
* 100 Museum Drive/ SR85, Shalimar
* 850/882 4062
* Daily 9:30–4:30
* Free

29D5

Florida Museum of Natural History

✉ Hull Road (off SW 34th Street)

☎ 352/846 2000

🕐 Mon–Sat 10–5, Sun and holidays 1–5

♿ Very good

✋ Free

Samuel P Harn Museum of Art

✉ Hull Road

☎ 352/392 9826

🕐 Tue–Fri 11–5, Sat 10–5, Sun 1–5

♿ Very good

✋ Free

Fine art adorns the galleries at the Samuel P. Harn Museum

28B5

🍴 Limited options ($–$$$)

Grayton Beach State Recreation Area

✉ CR30–A (off US98)

☎ 850/231 4210

🕐 Daily 8–dusk

✋ Cheap

GAINESVILLE ● ●

A pleasantly leafy university town, Gainesville is home to the University of Florida and its mighty Gators football team. Football weekends are to be avoided unless you are a fan, but otherwise head for the campus, where two of Gainesville's highlights are to be found.

First stop is the excellent **Florida Museum of Natural History**, which covers both the history and geography of the state. It has an excellent 6,000-square foot gallery devoted to pre-Columbia Calusa Indians and exhibits relating to Indian societies in the present day.

The neighboring and highly regarded **Samuel P. Harn Museum of Art** is another campus crown jewel with impressive collections of ancient and modern arts and crafts from Europe, Asia, Africa, and South America as well as the Chandler Collection of American Art. The collections have to be shown in rotation, and they frequently make way for high-profile traveling exhibitions.

Southwest of the town, the Kanapaha Botanical Gardens are a tranquil spot, with a hummingbird garden and woodland paths where spring flowers, azaleas, and camellias bloom early in the year. In summer, giant Amazon water lily pads float on the lake like 5ft-wide mattresses, and a tangle of honeysuckle, clematis, passion flowers, and jasmine wreathes the arches of the fragrant vinery.

Another interesting side trip is the Devil's Millhopper State Geological Site. The 500ft-wide natural sinkhole was caused by the collapse of the thin limestone crust covering an underground cavern. A 232-step staircase winds down into its cool 120ft-deep fern flanked recesses, which are watered by a dozen miniature waterfalls.

GRAYTON BEACH ●

A rare low-key seaside enclave on the Panhandle shore, with pine-shaded family vacation homes fronted by a magnificent stretch of beach. Preserved by the **Grayton Beach State Recreation Area**, it is often ranked in the top ten beaches in the U.S.

Just east of town, the whimsical Old Florida-style resort of Seaside is a local landmark and tourist attraction. Ostentatiously cute Victorian-inspired cottages with gingerbread trim and picket fences line the narrow red-brick paved paths, which are reserved for the use of spookily silent golf carts.

JACKSONVILLE ✪✪✪

Founded on the St. Johns River in 1822, and named for General Andrew Jackson, the first governor of Florida, Jacksonville is the huge and high-rise capital of the First Coast. This was the original tourist gateway to Florida, though today's visitors tend to head for the Jacksonville Beaches, 12 miles east of downtown, and visit the city's several attractions on day trips.

The heart of the city spans a bend in the river, with the business district and Jacksonville Landing shopping and restaurant complex on the north bank. It is linked to the 1¼-mile Riverwalk along the south bank by a water taxi service, which is a convenient route to the **Museum of Science and History**. This is the place to get to grips with the natural history of the state in Currents of Time, which charts 12,000 years of Jacksonville's story. Other exhibits include The Florida Naturalists Center displaying over 60 native species of animals and plants, plus The Universe of Science interactive exhibit.

➕ 29E5
🍴 Cafés/restaurants ($–$$$)
❓ Jacksonville Jazz Festival, Apr

Museum of Science and History

✉ 1025 Museum Circle
☎ 904/396 6674
🕐 Mon–Fri 10–5, Sat 10–6, Sun 1–6
♿ Very good
💰 Moderate

The sparkling Jacksonville city skyline

The Buccaneer Trail

The Buccaneer Trail follows the A1A coast road from the Jacksonville Beaches north to Fernandina Beach. The start point for this drive is the Mayport Ferry, which makes the short journey across the St. Johns River to Fort George Island every 30 minutes from 6:15AM to 10:15PM.

On reaching Fort George Island, turn right on the A1A. After 3 miles turn left and continue to the Kingsley Plantation.

Dating from 1798, Florida's oldest plantation home was bought by Zephaniah Kingsley in 1814. The plantation grew Sea Island cotton, sugar cane, citrus, and corn, and was worked by around 60 slaves. A neat row of 23 former slave quarters has survived in a clearing in the woods.

Fernandina's harbor shelters a fleet of shrimping boats

Turn left back onto A1A, and head north to the entrance to Little Talbot State Park.

This quiet natural preserve offers a choice of marsh and coastal hammock walks, and 5 miles of unspoiled beach dunes. Keep an eye out for otters and marsh rabbits, and the bird life which is plentiful and varied.

Continue northward on A1A, which crosses a causeway over the Nassau Sound to reach Amelia Island.

Amelia Island was named after George II's beautiful daughter during a brief period of English rule in 1735. Thirteen miles long and only 2½ miles wide at its broadest point, the island's beautiful beaches, and the pretty town of Fernandina Beach (➤ 76), make it one of Florida's most appealing low-key and relaxed vacation spots.

The quickest route back to the Jacksonville Beaches is to retrace your route down A1A south. Alternatively, take A1A west to join I–95 south for Jacksonville.

Distance
25 miles

Time
Allow a full day with stops

Start point
Mayport
➕ 29E5

End point
Fernandina Beach
➕ 29E5

Lunch
Marché Burette ($)
✉ Amelia Island Resort
☎ 904/261 6161

Decorative and fine art is exhibited in the galleries of the Cummer Museum

The **Cummer Museum of Art and Gardens** is worth the trip into Jacksonville alone. In the attractive Riverside residential district, it contains the finest art collection in the northeast, ranging from medieval and Renaissance European art to 20th-century American works, and from pre-Columbian antiquities to Meissen porcelain. The English and Italian gardens behind the museum face onto the river, shaded by a superb spreading live oak tree.

To the north of the city, **Jacksonville Zoo** has more than 800 animals and birds on show including Florida panthers, lions, elephants, giraffes, and apes. The newest area is the Range of the Jaguar, which comes complete with a large authentic rainforest environment. A minitrain chugs around the 73-acre site and there are regular animal encounter presentations.

On the banks of the St. Johns River, the **Fort Caroline National Memorial** marks the spot where French colonists attempted to establish a toehold in Florida in 1564. Timucua Indians helped the 300-man expeditionary force to build a wooden fort named after the French king, Charles IX, but it was destroyed by the Spanish the following year. Today there is an almost full-scale reproduction of the 16th-century fort, and woodland nature trails.

The Jacksonville Beaches stretch for around 25 miles south from Atlantic Beach down to the golfing resorts of Ponte Vedra Beach. The nicest section of oceanfront is in the **Kathryn Abbey Hanna Park**. Here, the beach is backed by dunes and a woodland nature preserve with walking and bicycle trails, fishing, and a campground.

Cummer Museum of Art and Gardens
- ✉ 829 Riverside Avenue
- ☎ 904/356 6857
- 🕐 Tue, Thu 10–9, Wed, Fri, Sat 10–5, Sun 12–5
- ♿ Very good
- 💰 Cheap

Jacksonville Zoo
- ✉ 8605 Zoo Parkway (off Heckscher)
- ☎ 904/757 4463
- 🕐 Daily 9–5
- ♿ Good
- 💰 Moderate

Fort Caroline National Memorial
- ✉ 12713 Fort Caroline Road
- ☎ 904/641 7155
- 🕐 Daily 9–5
- ♿ Good
- 💰 Free

Kathryn Abbey Hanna Park
- ✉ 500 Wonderwood Drive
- ☎ 904/249 4700
- 🕐 Daily 8–dusk
- ♿ Good
- 💰 Cheap

Food & Drink

The first rule of eating out in Florida is make sure you are hungry. From the awesome heights of an all-American breakfast to the mile-high Cuban sandwich at lunch and a fresh seafood dinner at the end of a busy day's sightseeing, Florida portion control errs well beyond the realms of simple generosity.

Sometimes you just have to eat with your fingers

Fresh seafood is always on the menu

Florida Specialities

In recent years, some of Florida's finest chefs have been perfecting "Floribbean" cuisine, a delicious fusion of fresh local produce and more exotic Caribbean flavours with a bit of New American and Asian flair thrown in. Otherwise, there are few typically Floridian dishes on the menu, but nobody should miss out on a chance to sample *real* Key lime pie, which should be yellow not green. Down in the Keys, conch fritters or chowder (a rather chewy seafood stew) are local dishes. Farmed alligator meat is usually served well disguised as deep-fried nuggets, but if it appears on the menu in a good restaurant it is well worth trying, and is not dissimilar to chicken.

In northern Florida there are plenty of opportunities to sample southern-style cooking. Grits (a sloppy cornmeal porridge best served with salt, pepper and butter) is something of an acquired taste, but barbecued meats are delicious, and look out for "blackened" dishes, which are coated with tangy Cajun-style spices.

Seafood

Seafood restaurants abound in Florida. Snapper, grouper, yellowtail, and pompano are among the top locally caught fish, and dolphin, also known as mahi-mahi, which is a fish not a performing mammal. In southern Florida, stone crabs are harvested from October to April, and in the Panhandle, shrimps, blue crabs, and oysters are local treats.

Cuban Cooking

The Latin American influence is strongest in the southern part of the state, particularly Miami. This is the place to sample a Cuban sandwich served in a long roll packed with cheese, ham, and pork, and a strong, sweet *café cubano*, a thimble-sized cup of coffee that more than lives up to its nickname: zoom juice. Favorite restaurant dishes include chicken with rice (*arroz con pollo*) and fried beef (*vaca frita*) served with black beans, rice, and fried plantain.

Hearty breakfasts served with a smile are the order of the day at this diner

Budget Bites

It is easy to eat out cheaply and well in Florida. Resort areas generally offer a wide choice of family restaurants and familiar fast food chains. Look out for special deals such as Early Bird menus served before the main evening rush, and all-you-can-eat fixed-price buffets. Larger shopping malls generally offer a food court with a selection of different cafés and take-away operations serving anything from pizza and deli sandwiches to Chinese and Tex-Mex dishes. Good ready-made meals and salads are sold in supermarkets, and buying up cold drinks at supermarket prices can save a small fortune.

A snappy advertisement for the local brew

Drinking

Soft drinks are widely available and vacationers should be sure to drink plenty in order to avoid dehydration in the hot Florida sunshine.

The legal drinking age is 21 and identification may be required as proof. Wine and beer are available in supermarkets, but liquor can only be bought in a liquor store.

28B5

Limited in Marianna; concession in the park

Florida Caverns State Park

✉ 3345 Caverns Road (off SR167)

☎ 850/482 9598

🕐 Daily 8–dusk (Mar–Sep 4:30)

Cheap

29D4

Café ($); restaurant ($$)

Marjorie Kinnan Rawlings State Historic Site

✉ CR325, Cross Creek

☎ 352/466 3672

🕐 Park daily 9–5; house tours Oct–May Thu–Sun 10, 11, 1, 2, 3, 4

♿ Good

Cheap

MARIANNA/FLORIDA CAVERNS STATE PARK

This state park offers a rare opportunity to explore Florida's limestone foundations through a series of stunning underground caverns. Around 65ft below ground, the caverns are decorated with eerily beautiful stalactites and stalagmites and maintain a cool 61–66°F. Above ground, there are woodland hiking trails and bridle paths, a swimming hole on the Chipola River, and a highly recommended 52-mile canoe trail, which follows the river south to the Apalachicola National Forest.

MICANOPY

The picture-perfect village of Micanopy with its old brick stores and Victorian homes dozes in the shade of magnificent live oaks planted in a canopy over Cholokka Boulevard. The store fronts may have been quietly hijacked by antiques and curio dealers and the grand Herlong Mansion transformed into a comfortable B&B, but this is a lovely corner of Old Florida. It is also a good base for a trip to the **Marjorie Kinnan Rawlings State Historic Site**, a fascinating Cracker homestead where the Pulitzer prizewinning writer lived during the 1930s and 1940s.

28A5

Café ($)

Blackwater River State Park

✉ 7720 Deaton Bridge Road, Holt. Off US90 (15 miles NE of Milton)

☎ 850/983 5363

🕐 Daily 8–dusk

Cheap

MILTON

Milton is the launch point for a selection of the finest canoeing trails in the state. Several operators (▶ 110) offer a wide range of options from half-day rowing and inner tube rides to three-day expeditions on the Coldwater and Blackwater rivers and Sweetwater and Juniper creeks. Canoe rental can also be arranged from outposts near **Blackwater River State Park**. Here there are hiking trails in the woodlands and swimming in the gently flowing sand-bottomed river, which has sandy beaches along its banks.

PANAMA CITY BEACH ⭐⭐

Chief resort of the "Redneck Riviera," so called for its enormous popularity with vacationers from the neighboring southern states, Panama City Beach fronts 27 miles of broad white sands with a wall of hotels, motels, and condominiums. Strung out along this "Miracle Strip" are amusement parks and arcades, miniature golf courses, shopping malls and family restaurants. Beachfront concessions offer a host of watersports activities, and there is excellent snorkeling and diving (► 110–11).

At the heart of the Strip is the Shipwreck Island Water Park, a popular alternative to the beach. It sits back to back with the bright lights and disco delights of the **Miracle Strip Amusement Park**, a nine-acre evening entertainment complex offering 30 fairground rides, from a giant roller coaster to swinging gondolas and a ferris wheel, plus cotton candy, carousels, and sideshows.

Panama City Beach has two animal attractions. **Gulf World** concentrates on the marine life side of things, with dolphin and sea lion shows, a walk-through shark tank, and assorted aquariums. The small, but evidently well-tended, **ZooWorld** attraction is home to more than 300 animals including bears, big cats, apes, and alligators. More than 15 of the animal species here are on the rare and endangered list. There is also a children's petting zoo.

A welcome escape from the busy main beach, **St. Andrews State Recreation Area** offers unspoiled dunes, woodland trails, fine swimming, and diving in the shallows. There are regular boat trips out to Shell Island for more lazing around on the beach or gentle shell collecting. Shell Island trips are also available from the Treasure Island and Captain Anderson's marinas.

✚ 28B5
🍴 Cafés/restaurants ($–$$$)

Miracle Strip Amusement Park
✉ 12000 Front Beach Road
☎ 850/234 5810
🕐 Daily Jun–Labor Day; Fri, Sat Apr–May
♿ Good
💷 Expensive

Gulf World
✉ 15412 Front Beach Road
☎ 850/234 5271
🕐 Daily from 9
♿ Good
💷 Expensive

ZooWorld
✉ 9008 Front Beach Road
☎ 850/230 1065
🕐 Daily 9–dusk
♿ Good
💷 Moderate

St. Andrews State Recreation Area
✉ 4607 State Park Lane, off Thomas Drive
☎ 850/233 5140
🕐 Daily 8–dusk
♿ Limited
💷 Cheap

Towers, verandas, and gabled roofs are features of the elegant homes built in Pensacola during the 19th century

---

➕ 28A5

🍴 Cafés/restaurants ($–$$$)

↔️ Milton (▶ 84)

🎉 Fiesta of Five Flags, Jun

Historic Pensacola Village

✉️ Visitor Center, 205 E Zaragoza Street

☎️ 850/595 5985

🕐 Mon–Fri 10–4

♿ Moderate

Fort Pickens National Park

✉️ 1400 Fort Pickens Road/SR399

☎️ 850/934 2635

🕐 Daily 8:30–dusk

♿ Good

♿ Moderate per car

The ZOO

✉️ 5701 Gulf Breeze Parkway

☎️ 850/932 2229

🕐 Daily 9–5

♿ Good

♿ Moderate

PENSACOLA ⭐⭐⭐

Spanish explorer Tristan de Luna made the first attempt to establish a colony at Pensacola in 1559, but the capital of the western Panhandle has to content itself with the title of second most historic town in Florida after St. Augustine. However, Pensacola does claim to be the "Cradle of Naval Aviation," and it is home to the excellent National Museum of Aviation (▶ 20).

The British laid out the city center in the 1770s, but most of the buildings in the **Historic Pensacola Village** date from the mid-19th-century timber boom era. A stroll around these tree-shaded streets and squares is a great way to spend half a day or so. There are small museums of local history, industry and commerce, a wealth of Victorian architecture, and tours around the interiors of a handful of restored homes.

Across Pensacola Bay, the seafront resort of Pensacola Beach has plenty for families and watersports enthusiasts. On the western tip of the barrier island, **Fort Pickens National Park** offers excellent swimming, hiking, and bicycle trails, and the massive five-sided early-19th century fort is open to the public.

East of Gulf Breeze **The ZOO** houses an exotic menagerie, including white Bengal tigers and snow leopards. The miniature train rides are fun for children and there is a very good petting area.

ST. AUGUSTINE (▶ 22, TOP TEN)

A Walk Around St. Augustine

The compact historic heart of St. Augustine (► 22) is the ideal size to explore on foot. This short walk starts from the 18th-century City Gates at the north end of St. George Street.

Lined with historic buildings, stores, and restaurants, St. George Street is the old city's main thoroughfare. Here the Oldest Wooden Schoolhouse (number 14) dates from around 1788, and the fascinating **Colonial Spanish Quarter** (number 33) depicts life in the 18th-century colonial town with the help of reconstructed buildings and a working blacksmith's shop. Peña-Peck House (number 143) was originally built for the Spanish Royal Treasurer in the 1740s, but it has been restored and furnished in mid-19th-century style.

At Plaza de la Constitucion, cut diagonally across to the right and take King Street. Cross Cordova Street.

On the right, Flagler College was once the grand Ponce de Leon Hotel, opened in 1888. Visitors are free to enter the lobby and peek into the elaborate Rotunda dining room.

Return to the Plaza and walk down the south side. Turn right on Aviles Street.

The Spanish Military Hospital (number 3) takes an unsentimental look at 18th-century medical practices.

Detour down Artillery Lane (on the right) for the Oldest Store Museum, or continue down Aviles Street to number 20.

The 1797 Ximenez-Fatio House was turned into a boarding house in the 1830s. It has been cleverly restored and each room is furnished in the appropriate style for a variety of 19th-century lodgers from a military man to a lady invalid.

Continue along Aviles. Turn left on Bridge Street, right on Charlotte Street, and left on St. Francis Street for the Oldest House.

Watch the blacksmith at work in St. Augustine

Distance
1 mile

Time
4 hours with stops

Start point
City Gates, St. George Street
✚ 29E5

End point
Oldest House, St. Francis Street
✚ 29E5

Lunch
Florida Cracker Café ($-$$)
✉ 81 St. George Street
☎ 904/829 0397

Spanish Colonial Quarter
✉ 33 St. George Street
☎ 904/825 6830
🕐 Daily 9–5:30
🎟 Moderate

✝ 28C5

🍴 Cafés/restaurants ($–$$$)

❓ Walk tour maps from the Visitors Center, New Capitol Building (West Plaza Level)

Old Capitol

✉ S Monroe Street at Apalachee Parkway

☎ 850/487 1902

🕐 Mon–Fri 9–4:30, Sat 10–4:30, Sun and holidays 12–4:30

♿ Good

🎟 Free

Museum of Florida History

✉ 500 S Bronough Street

☎ 850/245 0250

🕐 Mon–Fri 9–4:30, Sat 10–4:30, Sun and hols 12–4:30

♿ Very good

🎟 Free

Tallahassee Museum of History and Natural Science

✉ 3945 Museum Drive

☎ 850/575 8684

🕐 Mon–Sat 9–5, Sun 12:30–5

♿ Good

🎟 Moderate

A. B. Maclay State Gardens

✉ 3540 Thomasville Road/US319

☎ 850/487 4556

🕐 Park daily 8–dusk; gardens daily 9–5; house Jan–Apr 9–5

♿ Good

🎟 Cheap

Right: the Capitol Complex in the heart of Tallahassee

Facing page: a white heron stalks the reeds in Wakulla Springs State Park

TALLAHASSEE ✪✪

Diplomatically sited midway between the two historic cities of St. Augustine and Pensacola, the state capital is a fine old southern town just 14 miles from the Georgia border. Tallahassee radiates from the hilltop Capitol Complex, where the turn-of-the-last-century Old Capitol crouches in the shadow of its towering modern successor. Both are open to visitors, and the **Old Capitol** has a number of interesting historic exhibits.

It is a short stroll to the quiet tree-lined streets of the Park Avenue historic district where 19th-century legislators and merchants built gracious homes. Self-guided walk tour maps are available from the Capitol Complex visitor center and there are tours of the charming Knott House Museum in a restored 1840s house.

Another downtown attraction is the **Museum of Florida History**. Mastodon bones, historical dioramas, colonial, pioneer, and Civil War artifacts illustrate a colorful and informative potted history of the state. However, the museum most likely to appeal to young children is the terrific **Tallahassee Museum of History and Natural Science** out in the woods on the shores of Lake Bradford. Laid out in three main areas, the open-air

site contains Big Bend Farm, where volunteers in pioneer costume work the 1880s farm with its animals and crop gardens. Down by the water, a boardwalk trail leads past enclosures for Florida wildlife including bobcats and black bears. A third section preserves a selection of interesting historic buildings.

A favorite excursion from Tallahassee is a visit to the **A. B. Maclay State Gardens**, just north of the city. These glorious gardens were founded in the 1930s by Alfred B. Maclay, and surround his winter home. Naturally, the gardens look their best in the cooler months from December (when the first camellias bloom) until April. In the grounds there is boating on Lake Hall, woodland nature trails, and picnicking facilities.

WAKULLA SPRINGS STATE PARK ✪✪✪

South of Tallahassee, one of the world's biggest fresh-water springs bubbles up from the Florida aquifer into a 4½-acre pool at the center of the park. Snorkeling, swimming, and glass-bottomed boat rides provide a first-hand view of the underwater scenery and the water is so clear it is easy to see the bed of the pool 185ft below. Boat trips on the Wakulla River offer good wildlife-spotting opportunities. Look for alligators, deer, turtles, osprey, and a wide variety of wading birds.

✚ 28C5
✉ 550 Wakulla Park Drive/SR267 (off US319)
☎ 850/224 5920
◷ Daily 8–dusk
🍴 Concessions ($) and restaurant ($–$$)
♿ Good
💰 Cheap, boat tours cheap

WHITE SPRINGS ✪

A small town on the Suwannee River, White Springs' claim to fame is the **Stephen Foster State Folk Culture Center**. Born in Pennsylvania in 1826, Foster never even saw the Suwannee but he did make it famous with *Old Folks at Home* (► 73), or *Suwannee River*, which he wrote in southern dialect for a minstrel show in 1851.

In the park, a museum displays dolls' house dioramas depicting several of Foster's other famous songs such as *Oh! Susanna* and *Jeanie With The Light Brown Hair*, there are daily carillon recitals, craft shops, and pontoon boat rides on a pretty forest-lined stretch of the Suwannee.

✚ 29D5
✉ US41 N (3 miles E of I-95)
☎ 386/397 2733
◷ Daily 8–dusk; museum 9–5
🍴 Café ($)
♿ Good
💰 Cheap

Following page: *sailing into the sunset, just off Key West*

Where To...

Above: *colorful neon signs are designed to catch the eye*
Right: *Dixieland jazz at Rosie O'Grady's*

Miami

Prices

Prices are approximate, based on a three-course meal for one without drinks and service:

$ = under $15
$$ = $15–$30
$$$ = over $30

Diamond Ratings

As with the hotel ratings (► 100), AAA field inspectors evaluate restaurants on the overall quality of food, service, décor and ambiance – with extra emphasis given to food and service. Ratings range from one diamond (🌑) indicating a simple, family-oriented place to eat to five diamonds (🌑🌑🌑🌑🌑) indicating an establishment offering superb culinary skills and ultimate adult dining experience. Listings with **(N)** are AAA listed, but are awaiting evaluation.

A Warning

Many restaurants in Miami and other major cities have started to add an automatic service charge of around 15 percent to the bill. Check whether you have already been charged before counting out the tip.

Arnie and Richie's ($)

A local institution constructing deli sandwiches to die for, piled high with pastrami, cheese, rare roast beef, and other mouthwatering delicacies.
✉ 525 41st Street, North Miami Beach ☎ 305/531 7691
🕐 Breakfast, lunch, dinner

Astor Place Bar & Grill ($$$)

Amazing atrium setting for sophisticated fusion cuisine with Caribbean/Mediterranean influences such as pumpkin seed-crusted rack of lamb with mint salsa. The fried banana splits are famous.
✉ 956 Washington Avenue, Miami Beach ☎ 305/672 7217
🕐 Lunch, dinner

🌑🌑🌑 Balans ($–$$)

Terrific value for fashionable Lincoln Road Mall. Wide-ranging Mediterranean/Asian menu plus naughty-but-nice English desserts such as sticky toffee pudding. Outdoor seating offers an alternative to the ever-crowded interior.
✉ 1022 Lincoln Road, Miami Beach ☎ 305/534 9191
🕐 Breakfast, lunch, dinner

🌑🌑🌑 Café Prima Pasta ($$)

Be prepared to wait for a table at this excellent pasta place. Classic dishes are made with the freshest home-made pastas and sauces.
✉ 414 71st Street, North Miami Beach ☎ 305/867 0106
🕐 Lunch, dinner

🌑🌑 Café Tu Tu Tango ($$)

World food, from designer pizzas and Tex-Mex standards to Mediterranean salads and kebabs, dished up in a funky artist's loft setting.
✉ CocoWalk, 3015 Grand Avenue, Coconut Grove ☎ 305/529 2222 🕐 Lunch, dinner until late

🌑🌑🌑 China Grill ($$$)

Not Chinese cuisine but one of the best "world cuisine" restaurants in Miami. Popular with the in-crowd so who you are sitting next to is as important as the food.
✉ 404 Washington Avenue, South Beach ☎ 305/534 2211
🕐 Lunch and dinner

🌑🌑 Trattoria Da Leo ($$)

This popular Italian restaurant spills out onto the Lincoln Road Mall and makes a good lunch stop as well as an evening venue.
✉ 819 Lincoln Road, Miami Beach ☎ 305/674 0350
🕐 Lunch, dinner

Hard Rock Café ($$)

No surprises from the rock restaurant chain, but they still pack in the crowds for all the usual burgers, salads, and BLTs, with a side order of rock memorabilia.
✉ Bayside Marketplace, 401 Biscayne Boulevard
☎ 305/377 3110 🕐 Lunch, dinner until late

🌑🌑 Joe's Stone Crab ($$)

Opened in 1913 and the most renowned stone crab eatery in the city, Joe's is an unassuming place amid the famed SoBe clubs and bars.
✉ 11 Washington Avenue, Miami Beach ☎ 800 780 2722
🕐 Lunch Tue–Sat, dinner daily

🌑🌑 News Café ($)

An Ocean Drive landmark facing the beach. Outdoor

tables for prime people-watching and a leisurely brunch. Menu favorites include omelettes, salads, and pasta. Also at 2901 Florida Avenue, Coconut Grove (☎ 305/774 6397).

✉ **800 Ocean Drive, Miami Beach** ☎ **305/538 6397** ⓘ **24 hours**

☞☞☞ Nobu Miami Beach ($$$)
One of the "must visit" restaurants in SoBe, with a raft of celebrity clients. The sushi is excellent and décor is ultra chic.

✉ **1901 Collins Avenue (at the Shore Club)** ☎ **305/695 3100** ⓘ **Dinner daily**

☞☞☞ Normans ($$$)
Chef Norman Van Aken is considered one of the founders of "world cuisine," the fusion of North American, Latin, Caribbean and Asian styles of cooking. Fresh ingredients and a wood burning stove contribute to the exceptional flavors.

✉ **21 Almeria Avenue, Coral Gables** ☎ **305/446 6767** ⓘ **Dinner daily**

Orlando Seafood Restaurant & Fish Market ($)
Be prepared to enjoy your seafood on the hoof, as the Orlando is a stand-up affair. However, this minor inconvenience is reflected in the bargain prices for mouth-watering fish sandwiches and other treats.

✉ **501 NW 37th Avenue** ☎ **305/642 6767** ⓘ **Lunch, dinner**

Picnics at Allen's Drug Store ($)
It is Nostalgia City at this old-fashioned all-American diner, complete with a jukebox and ice-cream sodas. As befits such surroundings, the best bets are the home-cooked chilli, deli sandwiches, burgers, and Key lime pie.

✉ **4000 Red Road, South Miami** ☎ **305/665 6964** ⓘ **Breakfast, lunch, dinner**

☞☞☞ Restaurant St. Michel ($$$)
Excellent standards of service and an elegant dining room set the scene for the superb, French-influenced New American cuisine.

✉ **162 Alcazar Avenue, Coral Gables** ☎ **305/446 6572** ⓘ **Breakfast, lunch, dinner**

SoBe Bongo's Café ($$)
Cuban disco diva Gloria Estefan's great value Ocean Drive eatery (previously called Larios on the Beach) offers an alternative to Little Havana. Cuban sandwiches, beef dishes, black beans, and seafood paella for two are all worth investigating.

✉ **820 Ocean Drive, Miami Beach** ☎ **305/532 9577** ⓘ **Breakfast, lunch, dinner**

☞ Versailles ($$)
A legend in its own lifetime, this Little Havana institution is a sort of living slice of Latin American soap opera with food, serving up a massive menu of Cuban goodies to crowds of awestruck tourists and partying Cubanos dressed up to the nines. Lots of fun and open until late.

✉ **3555 SW 8th Street, Little Havana** ☎ **305/444 0240** ⓘ **Lunch, dinner**

The Cuban Cocktail
If you are dining out Cuban-style, go all Old Havana-colonial and order a round of *mojitos*. Made with white rum, lime juice, and a sprig of fresh mint, they are absolutely delicious and very refreshing. As well as wine and beer, most Cuban restaurants will also serve chilled *sangria*.

Southern Florida & the Florida Keys

Eating Hours

As a general rule, Florida's restaurants do not stay open late, particularly outside the major cities. Breakfast starts early—around 7; lunch lasts from around noon to 2:30; while dinner can start as early as 5:30 and be wrapped up by 9, though most resort area restaurants will serve until 10:30. Sunday brunch tends to run around 10–2.

Boca Raton

Flakowitz Bagel Inn ($)

This budget lunch stop is bagel heaven, where the Jewish deli roll is transformed into a well-filled work of art. There is a choice of meats, cheeses, and salads to either eat in or take away.

✉ **19999 N Federal Highway** ☎ **561/368 0666** 🕐 **Breakfast, lunch**

Mark's at the Park ($$–$$$)

Mark Militello is one of South Florida's most creative and successful chefs so don't miss the opportunity to sample his Floribbean/ Mediterranean cooking.

✉ **344 Plaza Real, Mizner Park** ☎ **561/395 0770** 🕐 **Lunch, dinner**

Fort Lauderdale

Black Orchid Café ($$$)

Set beside the intercoastal waterway, the Black Orchid offers a good range of dishes from chicken and seafood to unusual meats such as ostrich, buffalo, and game.

✉ **2980 North Ocean Boulevard** ☎ **954/561 9398** 🕐 **Dinner**

Café Italia ($$)

Authentic family owned Italian restaurant concentrating on northern Italian dishes and a good Italian wine list. Small outside terrace.

✉ **3471 North Federal Highway** ☎ **964/561 3900** 🕐 **Lunch, dinner**

Fort Myers

The Veranda ($$)

Housed in a pretty turn-of-the-19th-century historic home, the Veranda also offers courtyard dining in the summer months. The award-winning regional menu features fresh local produce.

✉ **2122 2nd Street** ☎ **941/332 2065** 🕐 **Lunch (except Sat), dinner. Closed Sun**

Islamorada

♛♛ Squid Row ($$)

Attracting accolades from many respected restaurant guides, and such former patrons as Elvis Presley and George Bush Senior, this is a great place for fresh fish and chargrilled steaks

✉ **81901 Overseas Highway** ☎ **305/664 9865** 🕐 **Lunch, dinner**

♛♛ Uncle's ($$)

Extensive menu focuses on fresh seafood, but there are lots of chicken, veal, pasta, salads, vegetarian and low fat options. They'll also cook your catch for you.

✉ **8090 Overseas Highway at Mile Marker 80.9** ☎ **305/664 4402** 🕐 **Dinner. Closed Sun**

Key Largo

♛♛♛♛ Frank Keys Café ($)

Gourmet dining in an unassuming little restaurant where interesting combinations include dishes based on seafood or prime cuts of lamb, steak and duck.

✉ **100211 Overseas Highway** ☎ **305/453-0310;** www.frankkeyscafe.com 🕐 **Dinner daily except Tue; lunch Mon and Wed–Fri.**

Mrs. Mac's Kitchen ($)

Join the locals at this landmark no-frills diner for the all-American breakfasts, fresh seafood, and generous daily specials. The dessert pies are a specialty.

✉ **Mile Marker 99.4** ☎ **305/451 3722** 🕐 **Breakfast, lunch, dinner. Closed Sun**

Key West

🍷🍷🍷 Antonia's ($$$)

This elegant Italian restaurant is a long-established feature of Key West's eating out scene. Traditional recipes are prepared by chef Phillip Smith using the best fresh ingredients.

✉ 615 Duval Street
☎ 305/294 6565;
www.antoniaskeywest.com
🍴 Dinner

🍷🍷 Blue Heaven ($$)

The motto is "No shoes, no shirt, no problem" at this laidback spot with trestle tables in the yard and a bathtub full of chilled beer on the bar. Generous helpings of Caribbean barbecue shrimp, chicken jerk, and grilled vegetable roulade.

✉ 729 Thomas Street
☎ 305/296 8666 🍴 Lunch, dinner

🍷 Pepe's ($)

Friendly local café-diner with outdoor tables in a tree-shaded garden. Hearty breakfasts, seafood, steaks, and barbecue.

✉ 806 Caroline Street
☎ 305/294 7192 🍴 Breakfast, lunch, dinner

🍷 Pisces ($$$)

Upscale seafood restaurant serving up succulent lobster and other *fruits de mer* in imaginative concoctions devised by chef Andrew Berman.

✉ 1007 Simonton Street
☎ 305/294 7100 🍴 Dinner

Naples

Bistro 21 ($$$)

Fusion cuisine with Mediterranean accents, concentrating on seafood combined with the freshest daily ingredients. A modern décor and low lighting offers a romantic ambience. Food is immaculately presented and you can order certain dishes as a "small plate" if you have a light appetite

✉ 821 5th Avenue South
☎ 239/261 5821 🍴 Dinner daily

Michelle-Marie's Restaurant on the Bay ($$$)

French cuisine in with views over Venetian Bay and a deck for outside dining. The menu bends toward Provençal but has some classics, including snails.

✉ 4236 Gulf Shore Boulevard North, The Village at Venetian Bay ☎ 239/263 0900
🍴 Lunch, dinner. Closed Sun May–Oct

Palm Beach

Leopard Lounge and Supper Club ($$$)

Leopard skin spots feature in the theatrical décor of this elegant supper club. Enjoy a tempting continental menu, excellent service and nightly entertainment.

✉ The Chesterfield Hotel, 363 Coconut Row ☎ 561/659 5800
🍴 Lunch, dinner

Sanibel and Captiva Islands

Lazy Flamingo II ($$)

A casual local spot with a nautical theme and the biggest bar on the island. There is a good selection of seafood, including a raw bar, plus burgers, prime rib sandwiches, and Caesar salad with grilled chicken.

✉ 1036 Periwinkle Way, Sanibel ☎ 239/472 6939
🍴 Lunch, dinner

Vegetarians

Vegetarians will not find dining out easy in Florida. It is simple to get by without red meat as most menus feature a few seafood dishes. But if you do not eat fish the choice tends to be very limited, leaving pasta, pizza, and salads (which tend to be pretty dire in budget restaurants).

Central Florida

Eating Out in the Theme Parks

All central Florida's major theme parks offer a variety of dining arrangements. Within SeaWorld, Universal Orlando, Busch Gardens, and the Walt Disney World parks the choice ranges from fast food concessions selling hamburgers, hot dogs, ice-cream, and cold drinks, to sandwich shops, cafés, and full-service restaurants. Reservations for the restaurants are advised and should be made at Guest Relations on entering the park or by contacting WDW at ☎ 407/WDW-DINE and Universal at ☎ 407/363 8000.

Clearwater Beach
🦀 Crabby Bill's ($–$$$)
Fresh seafood directly from the Gulf of Mexico is the basis of this renowned restaurant, the first in a chain of eight in Florida, just south of Clearwater. Stone crabs (in season) are a huge crowd puller but for non-fish fanciers there is steak, chicken and ribs.

✉ **401 Gulf Boulevard, Indian Rocks Beach** ☎ **727/595 4825**
🕐 **Lunch, dinner**

Cocoa Beach
Black Tulip ($$)
Cozy, fine dining restaurant in historic Cocoa Village. A Mediterranean influence can be detected in the pasta dishes or tuck into steak au poivre. Lunchtime options include soup and salads.

✉ **207 Brevard Avenue, Cocoa Village** ☎ **321/631 1133**
🕐 **Lunch, dinner**

Kissimmee
Angels ($–$$$)
Famed locally for its seafood buffet, this restaurant serves just about every type of American food—head here if your family can't agree on one particular style of cuisine.

✉ **7300 W Irlo Bronson Memorial Highway (at the Holiday Inn)** ☎ **407/397 1960**
🕐 **Breakfast, lunch, dinner**

Passage to India ($$)
Excellent Indian cuisine including a range of meats, tandoori, vegetarian, and vegan dishes served as hot as you like. Authentic Indian carved wood decoration in the dining room.

✉ **7618 E Irlo Bronson Memorial Highway** ☎ **863/424 6969** 🕐 **Lunch, dinner**

Ponderosa Steakhouse ($)
Family restaurant chain serving a very good value all-you-can-eat buffet laden with steak, chicken, seafood, bread, and salads.

✉ **5771 W Irlo Bronson Memorial Highway/US192** ☎ **407/397 2100** 🕐 **Breakfast, lunch, dinner**

Orlando
💎💎 Bahama Breeze ($$)
One of the few places on I-Drive where you can eat outside on their deck. Mexican, Cuban, and Thai dishes make tasty appetizers while the full menu features the same with American meat and seafood options. Live reggae and Caribbean music nightly. You must be over 21 to be on the deck after 9PM or be accompanied by an adult.

✉ **8849 International Drive** ☎ **407/248 2499** 🕐 **Dinner (from 4PM).**

💎💎💎 Delfino Riviera ($$$)
Authentic Ligurian Italian cuisine based around seafood dishes served on Versace designed tableware, with views over Orlando's interpretation of Portofino Bay. Italian minstrels complete the Mediterranean atmosphere.

✉ **6501 Universal Boulevard, Portofino Bay Hotel** ☎ **407/503 1010 or 888/273 1311**
🕐 **Dinner Tue–Sat**

💎💎💎 The Palm ($$$)
The great Palm steakhouse family owned group has found a home in Orlando. Perfectly cooked fillets and chops, plus chicken, seafood and salads, in an upscale family oriented ambiance.

5800 Universal Boulevard at the Hard Rock Hotel
☎ 407/503 7256 ⏰ Dinner

♨♨ Race Rock ($$)
Striking car racing-themed décor, complete with whole cars, bikes and giant trucks, plus pumping rock music and a mile-long menu featuring burgers, pizzas, pasta, Tex-Mex, and more.
✉ 8986 International Drive
☎ 407/248 9876 ⏰ Lunch, dinner

St. Pete Beach
♨♨ Sea Critters Café ($–$$)
Casual dockside dining on the waterfront deck or indoors. Tasty menu includes hot fish sandwiches, seafood pasta, Cajun blackened chicken salad, and Jamaican jerk.
✉ 2007 Pass-a-Grille Way
☎ 727/360 3706 ⏰ Lunch, dinner

♨♨ Leverock's ($$)
One of ten locations in Florida. Here you can gaze out at the sea while you eat succulent seafood so fresh that was out there swimming around just a short while ago. There are a few meat dishes on the menu too.
✉ 10 Corey Avenue ☎ 727/367-4588 ⏰ Lunch, dinner

Sarasota
Chef Caldwell's ($$$)
A delicious choice of New American, Floribbean and Mediterranean ideas such as tomato-based conch chowder, Maryland crab cakes, rack of lamb, and vegetarian pasta.
✉ 20 S Adams Drive (off St Armands Circle) ☎ 941/388 5400 ⏰ Lunch, dinner. Closed Tue

Gulf Drive Café ($–$$)
Cheap and cheerful casual dining on the waterfront. This is the best kind of breakfast-served-any-time café. In addition to omelettes, sandwiches and burgers, there are more substantial evening meals.
✉ 900 Gulf Drive, Bradenton Beach ☎ 941/778 1919
⏰ Breakfast, lunch, dinner

Tampa
♨♨♨ Bern's Steak House ($$$)
Seriously juicy prime steaks and fresh organic vegetables are the trademark of this famously comfortable and clubby local legend. Reservations are recommended.
✉ 1208 S Howard Avenue
☎ 813/251 2421 ⏰ Dinner

Walt Disney World® Resort
Hoop-Dee-Doo Musical Revue ($$$)
This country-style hoe-down and all-you-can-eat barbecue is one of the most popular Disney dining experiences (▶ panel).
✉ Disney's Fort Wilderness Resort, 4510 N Fort Wilderness Trail ☎ 407/939 3462
⏰ Dinner

Rainforest Café ($$–$$$)
An amusement park attraction in its own right, this entertaining jungle-themed restaurant in a mini volcano provides its own micro-climate and wildlife, as well as an American menu with a Caribbean twist (▶ panel).
✉ Downtown Disney (Village Marketplace), 1800 E Buena Vista Drive ☎ 407/933 2800
⏰ Lunch, dinner

Disney Character Dining
Even the pickiest child eaters tend to toe the line when promised a date with Mickey Mouse. Disney character dining opportunities kick off at breakfast time when Donald hosts proceedings at Restaurantosaurus in Disney's Magic Kingdom. Throughout the day there are character appearances concluding with dinner where Mickey rules the roost at Chef Mickey's at Disney's Contemporary Resort. For current schedules and reservations ☎ 407/939 3463.

Northern Florida

Oystering in Apalachicola

Around 90 percent of Florida's oyster catch is harvested in Apalachicola Bay. Local oystermen are known as "tongers" for the scissor-like long-handled tools they use to prise their catch from the oyster beds in the sheltered bay. Oysters can be gathered throughout the year, but must reach a minimum length of 3in before they can be sent to market.

Apalachicola
Apalachicola Seafood Grill and Steakhouse ($–$$)

Sample the best of local seafood from oyster stew to smoked oysters, whopper fish sandwiches to the all-you-can-eat fried fish basket.
⊠ 100 Market Street
☎ 850/653 9510 🕐 Lunch, dinner

Cedar Key
Blue Desert Café ($)

Kitsch southwestern décor in an old shotgun cottage just east of town, and a long and varied menu of delicious sandwiches, pizzas, pasta, and knock-out dessert pies.
⊠ 12518 SR24 ☎ 352/543 9111 🕐 Dinner until late. Closed Sun–Mon

Island Hotel ($$)

This historic inn specializes in fresh seafood straight off the docks; local treats include blue crabs and clams. Check out the murals in the bar.
⊠ 373 2nd Street ☎ 352/543 5111 🕐 Lunch (weekends only), dinner. Closed Tue

Daytona Beach
🐝🐝 Hungarian Village ($–$$)

Authentic Hungarian cuisine is the specialty of this unusual restaurant. Dishes such as chicken paprika feature a delicious combination of flavors, and the home-made breads are wonderful.
⊠ 127 South Ocean Avenue
☎ 386/253 5224 🕐 Lunch, dinner

Destin/Fort Walton Beach
Fudpuckers ($$)

A little bit of everything in this American tropical island style eatery with a range of snacks, meals, and a sushi bar. There's a huge screen TV for sports lovers and you can feed gators off the deck!
⊠ 20001 Emerald Coast Highway ☎ 850/654 4200
🕐 Lunch, dinner

Fernandina Beach
🐝🐝🐝 Beech Street Grill ($$$)

A nest of attractive modern dining rooms in a charming old property in the historic district. Innovative New American cooking with local seafood, and a good wine list.
⊠ 801 Beech Street
☎ 904/277 3662 🕐 Dinner

🐝🐝🐝🐝 Florida House Inn ($)

All-you-can-eat boarding house dinners served up in Florida's oldest hotel (► 103). Trestle tables are loaded with home-cooked southern food.
⊠ 20–22 S 3rd Street
☎ 904/261 3300 🕐 Lunch (Tue–Sat), dinner

Gainesville
Panache at the Wine and Cheese Gallery ($)

This deli café makes an ideal lunch stop with outdoor patio tables for fine weather. Choose from a good selection of home-made soups and salads, sandwiches and fine cheeses.
⊠ 113 N Main Street
☎ 352/372 8446 🕐 Lunch, dinner

Jacksonville
🐝🐝 Dolphin Depot ($$)

Very popular and very good seafood restaurant noted for its excellent daily specials. The Depot dolphin fish with matchstick sweet potatoes and home-made chutney is a house specialty.

✉ 704 N 1st Street, Jacksonville Beach ☎ 904/270 1424 🕓 Dinner

Southend Brewery & Smokehouse ($$)

A water's edge restaurant with a micro-brewery at its heart and the tantalizing aroma of the smokehouse. Hearty racks of ribs, ale-steamed sausages and BBQ dishes, rich pies and brownies. Specialty beers.

✉ Jacksonville Landing ☎ 904/665 0000 🕓 Lunch, dinner

Panama City Beach

Capt Anderson's ($$–$$$)

Great harborfront location for one of the best restaurants in town. Seafood heads up the menu, and the Greek salads are a specialty.

✉ 5551 N Lagoon Drive ☎ 850/234 2225 🕓 Dinner

Couzins Country Cookin' Buffet ($)

The largest buffet in the area concentrates on all-American fayre including fried chicken, catfish and pot roast – something for everyone

✉ 7715 Front Beach Road ☎ 850/230 3568 🕓 Breakfast, lunch, dinner

Pensacola

Dharma Blue ($$)

Set in a pretty clapboard house with tables also in the garden, Dharma Blue serves American, Mediterranean and Asian dishes with a choice of lunchtime snacks and sandwiches as well as full entrées.

✉ 300 South Alcaniz Street ☎ 850/433 1275 🕓 Lunch, dinner Mon–Sat

🍷🍷🍷 **Jaime's ($$$)**

Lovely historic home, with an art deco interior and classy wide-ranging menu drawing on Floribbean and continental influences.

✉ 424 E Zaragoza Street ☎ 850/434 2911 🕓 Dinner. Closed Sun

🍷🍷 **McGuire's Irish Pub ($)**

A good atmosphere, a busy bar and home-brewed beers. Ribs, burgers, seafood, and other favorites on the menu.

✉ 600 E Gregory Street ☎ 850/433 6789 🕓 Lunch, dinner

St. Augustine

Cap's on the Water ($–$$)

A friendly and unpretentious local bar and restaurant with a rustic interior. Excellent seafood served Southern style and Florida specials such as gator tail.

✉ 4325 Myrtle Road, North Beach ☎ 904/824 8794 🕓 Lunch, dinner

🍷🍷🍷 **Raintree ($$$)**

Pretty setting in a restored historic building, friendly service, and a well-balanced menu that includes plenty of fresh seafood and notable home-made desserts.

✉ 102 San Marco Avenue ☎ 904/824 7211 🕓 Dinner

Tallahassee

🍷🍷🍷 **Chez Pierre($$$)**

Special occasion dining in a fine old building, where several dining areas with bold color schemes create a classy ambience. The French cuisine is very special too

✉ 1215 Thomasville Road ☎ 850/222-0936 🕓 Lunch Mon–Sat, dinner daily, except Sun in summer. Sun brunch.

Dining with Children

Families traveling with young children can breathe a sigh of relief when they arrive in Florida. The states' child-friendly attitude extends to restaurants of all descriptions. Staff will usually make great efforts to see that children are welcomed and children's menus are widely available; if you do not see one on display, always ask.

Miami

Diamond Ratings

AAA field inspectors evaluate and rate lodging establishments based on the overall quality and services. AAA's diamond rating criteria reflect the design and service standards set by the lodging industry, combined with the expectations of members.

Properties rated with one (![diamond]) or two (![diamonds]) diamonds are clean and well-maintained, offering comfortable rooms, with the two diamond property showing enhancements in décor and furnishings. A three (![diamonds]) diamond property shows marked upgrades in physical attributes, services and comfort and may offer additional amenities. A four (![diamonds]) diamond rating signifies a property offering a high level of service and hospitality and a wide variety of amenities and upscale facilities. A five (![diamonds]) diamond rating represents a world-class facility, offering the highest level of luxurious accommodations and personalized guest services.

Useful Websites

www.biltmorehotel.com
Delano Hotel – no website
www.doralresort.com
www.hamptoninn.com
www.mandarin-oriental.com
www.miamiriverinn.com
www.mutinyhotel.com
www.wyndham.com

♦♦♦♦♦ Biltmore Hotel ($$$$)

Luxurious 1920s Mediterranean Revival-style landmark with grand public rooms and spacious accommodations. There is an excellent restaurant; a magnificent outdoor pool, tennis, and golf.

✉ **1200 Anastasia Avenue, Coral Gables** ☎ **305/445 1926 or 1-800 727 1926**

Delano Hotel ($$$)

One of Miami's coolest hotels strikes a pose on the oceanfront. The decor is minimalist chic, the atmosphere superior, and the restaurant very good. Pool and fitness center.

✉ **1685 Collins Avenue, Miami Beach** ☎ **305/672 2000 or 1-800 555 5001**

♦♦♦♦ Doral Golf Resort and Spa ($$–$$$)

A place to suit golfers and their families, with five championship courses – it's hosted the PGA Tour since 1962 – and a luxury spa. There's also a superb water park and program of children's activities.

✉ **4400 87th Avenue** ☎ **305/592-2000 or 1-800 713 6725**

♦♦♦ Hampton Inn ($$)

This mainland hotel provides a convenient base for sight-seeing, shopping, and dining in the Grove. There is a pool and the tariff includes breakfast.

✉ **2800 SW 28th Terrace, Coconut Grove** ☎ **305/448 2800**

♦♦♦♦♦ Mandarin Oriental ($$)

This is one of the best hotels in the U.S.A., offering superlative luxury, superb amenities and the highest levels of service. Rooms are cool and sophisticated, and each has a marble bathroom and a spacious balcony overlooking Biscayne Bay. There's a three-story spa and a health and fitness center, a private beach and a range of organized activities. The restaurant, under star chef Michelle Bernstein, has won many awards.

✉ **500 Brickell Key Drive** ☎ **305/913-8288 or 866 888 6780**

♦♦ Miami River Inn ($$)

A lovely 40-room hotel in Little Havana with lots of character, including hardwood floors and antique-furnished rooms. There's an outdoor pool and spa tub.

✉ **118 SW South River Drive** ☎ **305/305-0045 or 1-800 468-3589**

♦♦♦ Mutiny Hotel ($$–$$$)

Suite-only boutique hotel in the Coconut Grove area of the city close to shopping, cafés, restaurants, and clubs. All rooms have modern kitchens and English colonial designed rooms. Upper stories have excellent views over Sailboat Bay or the city. There's a fitness room, spa, and pool.

✉ **2951 South Bayshore Drive** ☎ **305/441 2822**

♦♦♦ Wyndham Miami Beach Resort ($$$)

This huge, refurbished hotel is right on the oceanfront and offers excellent watersports facilities. It is particularly good for families with children.

✉ **4833 Collins Avenue, Miami Beach** ☎ **305/532 3600 or 1-800 221 8844**

Southern Florida & the Florida Keys

Islamorada

 Cheeca Lodge ($$$)
Quiet, low-rise resort complex on the oceanside. Excellent fishing and diving, children's programs, and gourmet dining.
✉ **Mile Marker 82.5** ☎ **305/664 4651 or 1-800 327 2888**

Sands of Islamorada ($$-$$$)
An attractive waterfront resort with a pier for boating, fishing and snorkeling, a swimming pool and a hot tub under the palm trees.
✉ **80051 Overseas Highway** ☎ **305/664-2791 or 888 741 4518**

Key Largo

Marina Del Mar Resort and Marina ($-$$$)
All kinds of water-based fun, including diving, boat rentals, fishing and swimming with dolphins. All rooms have balconies with marina views.
✉ **527 Caribbean Drive** ☎ **305/451-4107 or 1-800 451 3483**

Rock Reef Resort ($-$$)
Family-owned waterfront resort with verdant gardens, palm-shaded hammocks and private sandy beach. Rooms, efficiencies, apartments and cottages are available.
✉ **97850 Overseas Highway** ☎ **305/852-2401 or 1-800 477 2343**

Key West

Cypress House ($$-$$$)
Set in an 1888 traditional 'conch' house, this grand B&B is only one block from the excitement of Duval Street. There's a swimming pool and rooms have A/C. Excellent continental breakfast and cocktail hour included in the price.
✉ **601 Caroline Street** ☎ **305/294 6969**

The Watson House ($$-$$$)
Beautiful bed-and-breakfast in a fine 1860 house, set in lovely gardens. The three suites and cabana are all uniquely decorated, some with modern designer furniture, some with antique pieces and original art works.
✉ **525 Simonton Street** ☎ **305/294-6712 or 1-800 621 9405**

Naples

Ritz Carlton Naples ($$$)
The height of luxury, set on the fabulous Naples beach, with its own spa, golf, tennis, and watersports facility plus the usual pools and fitness center. The resort has seven restaurants. Rooms are plush.
✉ **280 Vanderbilt Beach Road** ☎ **239/598 3300**

Palm Beach

The Breakers ($$$)
Palatial hotel originally built by Henry Flagler in 1896, but rebuilt in 1925 after a fire. It offers the ultimate luxury and unparalleled service.
✉ **1 S County Road** ☎ **561/655-6611 or 1-888 273 2537; fax: 561/659-8403**

Captiva Island

South Seas Plantation ($$$)
Large, attractively landscaped resort with hotel rooms, condos and cottages, beach, pools and marina.
✉ **5400 Plantation Road, Captiva** ☎ **239/472 5111 or 1-800 449 1827**

Prices

Prices are for a double room during the high season (see panel opposite), excluding breakfast and taxes:

$	= under $100
$$	= $100-$180
$$$	= over $180

Hotel bills are subject to a six percent Florida sales tax and variable local resort taxes.

Seasonal Variations

Room prices can vary dramatically from season to season in Florida. In central and southern Florida, and the Florida Keys, the high season is December to April. During summer room rates can drop by as much as 40 percent, and it is well worth bargaining if you have not paid for your accommodations in advance. In the north, high season rates apply from October to April. It is worth bearing in mind that Florida is a popular family destination and vacation periods can be busy.

Useful Websites

www.cheeca.rockresorts.com
www.sandsofislamorada.com
www.marinadelmarkeylargo.com
www.rockreefresort.com
www.cypresshousekw.com
www.bestonkeywest.com
www.ritzcarlton.com
www.thebreakers.com
www.southseasplantation.com

Central Florida

Reservations

Reservations can be made by telephone, fax, email or mail, and should be made as early as possible in high season (➤ 101, panel) and vacation periods. A deposit (usually by credit card) equivalent to the nightly rate will ensure your room is held until 6PM; if you are arriving later inform the hotel. Credit card is the preferred payment method in most hotels. Payment by traveler's checks or cash may have to be made in advance.

Useful Websites

www.palmpavilion.com
http://mainstaysuites.orbitz.com
www.qualitysuitesmaingate.com
www.bestwesternplaza.com
www.hardrock.com
www.sirata.com
www.disney.com

Clearwater Beach

💎💎 Palm Pavilion Inn ($$)

Right on the Gulf of Mexico, this attractive hotel has various types of rooms, suites and apartments, with amenities that include TV, dataport and safe.

✉ 421 Hamden Drive
☎ 727/461 4862

Kissimmee

💎💎💎 MainStay Suites ($–$$)

Simple, suites-only property made special by its location on the banks of a natural lake with reeds, birdlife and a small natural beach. All suites have a kitchenette. Shuttles to the Disney parks.

✉ 4786 West Irlo Bronson Memorial Highway ☎ 407/396 2056

💎💎💎 Quality Suites Maingate East ($$)

Good family hotel with one- or two-bedroom suites with kitchens around a quadrangle with a pool. Continental breakfast and Disney shuttle included. In walking distance of Old Town entertainment/ shopping complex.

✉ 5876 Irlo Bronson Memorial Highway ☎ 407/396 8040

Orlando

💎💎💎 Best Western Plaza International ($$)

Modern chain hotel with rooms and family suites. Good children's facilities and babysitting service.

✉ 8738 International Drive
☎ 407/345 8195 or 1-800 654 7160

💎💎💎 💎💎💎 Hard Rock Hotel ($$$)

The rock themed hotel/café chain worked with Universal

to create this huge complex. Excellent amenities within walking distance of the two theme parks.

✉ 5800 Universal Boulevard
☎ 800-BE-A-STAR

St. Pete Beach

💎💎💎💎 Sirata Beach Resort ($$)

Big beachfront property with spacious rooms, a restaurant, lively tiki bar, and pool. Watersports rentals are available.

✉ 5300 Gulf Boulevard
☎ 727/363-5100 or 1-800 344 5999

💎💎💎 Trade Winds Sandpiper ($$)

A large hotel in a superb beachfront location. Of the variety of rooms and suites available, the best are those with picture windows and balconies overlooking the Gulf of Mexico.

✉ 6000 Gulf Boulevard
☎ 727/360-5551 or 1-800 237 0707

Walt Disney World® Resort

💎💎💎 Disney's All-Star Sports, Movie and Music Resorts ($–$$)

Three good value themed resorts with sporting, movie or musical motifs.

✉ 1701-1801 W Buena Vista Lake Drive ☎ All-Star Sports. 407/939 5000; All-Star Music, 407/939 6000; reservations, 407/934 7639

💎💎💎 Disney's Caribbean Beach Resort ($$)

Large, comfortable rooms in five tropically landscaped "villages," each boasting a pool and lakeside beach.

✉ 900 Cayman Way
☎ 407/934 3400; reservations, 407/934 7639

Northern Florida

Apalachicola

🐚🐚🐚 **Coombs House Inn ($–$$)**

Lovely Victorian B&B in a grand old home furnished with antiques (some four-poster beds) and within walking distance of stores and restaurants. Some rooms in a cottage across the street.

✉ **80 6th Street** ☎ **850/653 9199**

Daytona Beach

🐚🐚🐚 **Inn on the Beach ($–$$)**

Great value accommodations right on the beach. Rooms, suites and efficiencies all have sea views, and are equipped with microwave and refrigerator, cable TV and VCR, coffee-maker (with free coffee) and voice mail. Free daily newspaper and continental breakfast.

✉ **1615 Atlantic Avenue, Daytona Beach Shores** ☎ **386/255-0921 or 1-800 874 0975**

Fernandina Beach

🐚🐚🐚🐚 **Amelia Island Plantation ($$$)**

A superb resort property set in 1,000 acres of woodland, beach dunes and golf courses. Lavishly furnished and attractive hotel rooms, condos and villas, fine dining and matchless facilities.

✉ **3000 First Coast Highway** ☎ **904/261 6161 or 888/261 6161**

🐚🐚🐚 **Florida House Inn ($$)**

Lovingly restored historic B&B inn in the center of town, with 11 rooms, a restaurant (► 98), and a garden. In the evening, the friendly bar is a local favorite.

✉ **20–22 S 3rd Street** ☎ **904/261 3300**

Pensacola

🐚🐚 **Ramada Inn Bayview ($$)**

In a secluded setting by the bay, this hotel is arranged around a central swimming pool within leafy gardens. Each of the 150 rooms has a private balcony or patio. Complimentary airport transportation is available.

✉ **333 Fort Pickens Road** ☎ **850/932 3536 or 1-800 833 8637**

St. Augustine

🐚🐚 **Bayfront Inn ($–$$)**

Right on the waterfront, this Spanish-style inn with a pool is also close to the historic district attractions, stores, and restaurants

✉ **138 Avenida Menendez** ☎ **904/824 1681 or 1-800 558 3455**

🐚🐚🐚🐚 **Casa Monica ($$)**

In the heart of the old city, this landmark 1888 building looks just like a Spanish castle – and counts the King and Queen of Spain among its visitors. It combines impeccable service with a truly welcoming atmosphere, and rooms are individually furnished.

✉ **95 Cordova Street** ☎ **904/827-1888 or 1-800 648 1888**

Tallahassee

🐚🐚🐚 **La Quinta Inn ($)**

Attractive inn just 2 miles (3.2km) from downtown and is a great place to relax, perhaps by the swimming pool, after a day in the city. The continental breakfast buffet is complimentary.

✉ **2905 Monroe Street** ☎ **850/385 7172 or 1-800 432 9755; fax: 850/878-6665**

Bed and Breakfast

Florida's B&B inns make a lovely change from the big resort hotels. Most B&Bs are in restored historic homes and the rooms are individually furnished with antiques. In some places mod cons such as television have been banished. Breakfasts are usually huge and feature delicious home-cooked breads and pastries, cereals, eggs and bacon, cheeses and fresh fruit. If you are travelling with the family, check ahead, as some places do not accept children under 12.

Useful Websites

www.coombshouseinn.com
www.innonthebeach.com
www.aipfl.com
www.floridahouseinn.com
www.ramadabayview.com
www.bayfrontinn.com
www.casamonica.com
www.laquinta.com

Shopping Districts & Malls

Souvenir Suggestions

Florida is the capital of kitsch and just the place to pick up flashing flamingo Christmas lights, an alligator-shaped ashtray, or a can of Florida sunshine. T-shirt bargains abound, but do check for quality; Western wear, such as cowboy boots, check shirts, and belts, is also popular. Sponges and sea shells from the Gulf of Mexico are light and easy to pack. On the food front, citrus candies and jams, Key lime products from the Florida Keys, hot sauce, and barbecue marinades bring home the taste of Florida.

Sales Tax

Though shopping in Florida is generally a bargain for overseas visitors, be prepared for the local sales tax, which is not included in the displayed price. Sales tax varies from county to county, but averages around 6 percent, and will be added to the bill at the point of sale.

Miami

Bal Harbour Shops

A luxurious collection of European designer boutiques and the top US department stores Neiman Marcus and Saks Fifth Avenue in Miami's most exclusive shopping mall.

✉ **9700 Collins Avenue, Miami Beach** ☎ **305/866 0311**

Bayside Marketplace
(➤ 32)

CocoWalk

Boutiques, bistros, and souvenirs at the heart of the fun Coconut Grove shopping district. More of the same (plus a great bookstore) at The Streets of Mayfair, 2911 Grand Avenue.

✉ **3015 Grand Avenue, Coconut Grove** ☎ **305/444 0777**

Lincoln Road Mall

This funky pedestrian street boasts an entertaining mixture of art galleries, boutiques and specialty stores from designer lighting emporiums to hand-rolled cigars. Restaurants and sidewalk cafés revive weary shoppers.

✉ **924 Lincoln Road, Miami Beach** ☎ **305/531 3442**

Southern Florida and the Florida Keys

Boca Raton
Royal Palm Plaza

Appropriately clad in pretty pink stucco, this attractive open-air mall harbors around 80 chic little boutiques, jewelers, galleries, beauty salons, and cafés.

✉ **N Federal Highway/US1 (south of Palmetto Park Road)** ☎ **561/447 0008**

Fort Lauderdale
Las Olas Boulevard

This attractive downtown shopping street is well stocked with boutiques and galleries. The new Las Olas Riverfront shopping and dining complex overlooks the New River.

✉ **Las Olas Boulevard** ☎ **1-888-4-LASOLAS**

Key West
Duval and Simonton Streets

While Duval is Key West's busiest shopping street, there are a couple of factory stores on Simonton. Check out the tropical prints at Key West Fabrics and Fashions (number 201); and the designs at The T-Shirt Factory (number 316).

Naples
Third Street South and the Avenues

This charming small shopping and dining enclave offers a tempting selection of contemporary fashion and resort wear boutiques, modern art galleries, and specialty shops.

✉ **3rd Street S (between Broad and 14th Avenues S)** ☎ **941/649 6707**

Palm Beach
Worth Avenue

Small but perfectly formed, and great for window-shopping, the upscale shopping enclave of Worth Avenue comprises four gracious little blocks lined with a collection of the world's most expensive designer boutiques, art galleries, and jewelers.

✉ **Worth Avenue (between S Ocean Boulevard and Coconut Row)** ☎ **561/659 6090**

West Palm Beach
The Gardens Mall
An enormous indoor mall with more than 160 stores and restaurants. The Gardens also contains a food court and five department stores, including Macy's, Bloomingdale's, Sears, and Saks Fifth Avenue.

✉ **3101 PGA Boulevard, Palm Beach Gardens** ☎ **561/775 7750**

Central Florida

Cocoa/Cocoa Beach
Historic Cocoa Village
This quiet little corner of old Cocoa boasts an appealing selection of craft shops, gift stores, boutiques, and cafés laid out along brick-paved sidewalks and shady lanes.

✉ **Brevard Avenue (S of SR520)** ☎ **321/631 9075**

Merritt Square Mall
Space Coast shopping and entertainment complex.

✉ **777 E Merritt Island Causeway/SR520** ☎ **321/452 3272**

Kissimmee
Old Town Kissimmee
There is all the fun of the fair at this Old West style open-air mall, which offers around 70 souvenir stores, clothing and gift shops, plus dining and fairground amusement rides to entertain children.

✉ **5770 W Irlo Bronson Memorial Highway/US192** ☎ **407/396 4888**

Orlando
Mall at Millenia
The most up-market mall in Orlando with Macy's and Bloomingdale's department stores plus a range of fine boutiques from Tiffany to Chanel.

✉ **4200 Conroy Road** ☎ **407/363 3555**

Florida Mall
Central Florida's largest and most popular shopping destination with over 250 stores and restaurants and five department stores including Saks Fifth Avenue. Most of the top U.S. brand-name fashion stores are here and there is a well-stocked Warner Bros Studio Store.

✉ **8001 S Orange Blossom Trail/US441** ☎ **407/851 6255**

Park Avenue
The smart Orlando suburb of Winter Park offers a relaxing alternative to the big shopping malls. Browse in the fashionable boutiques, gifts, crafts and art galleries along the avenue.

✉ **Park Avenue at New York Avenue** ☎ **407/629 0042**

St. Petersburg
The Pier
More of a sightseeing feature than a major shopping experience, but very popular nonetheless. A variety of small boutiques and stores sell fashion, gifts, and souvenirs. There is also dining with waterfront views.

✉ **800 2nd Avenue NE** ☎ **727/821 6443**

Sarasota
St. Armands Circle
Downtown has The Quay mall, but St. Armands Circle's collection of upscale boutiques, galleries, specialty stores and cafés is much more tempting.

✉ **St. Armands Key (SR789)** ☎ **941/388 1554**

The Great Merchandise Heist
If theme park admission were not enough to seriously dent your wallet, dozens of tempting merchandise outlets make it easy to spend a second unscheduled fortune on T-shirts, cuddly toys and other must-have souvenirs. One way to avoid this pitfall is to make a deal with children about what they can expect to take home, and stick to it. Visitors to Walt Disney World can save valuable sightseeing time by shopping at the one-stop World of Disney superstore (▶ 106).

Antiques and Collectibles

Several Florida towns boast antiques districts which can be really fun to explore, though the goods on sale could be described more accurately as bric-à-brac. Genuine Victoriana includes dolls, linens, glass, and small furnishings. "Collectibles" covers everything else, from the contents of the attic and the garage to entertaining Florida souvenirs of the 1920s and 30s.

Tampa

International Plaza

Almost 200 stores and Bay Street outdoor village with a range of restaurants and cafés make this mall a little different from others in Tampa.

✉ **Corner of Boy Scout Boulevard and West Shore Boulevard** ☎ 813/342 3790

Old Hyde Park Village

This attractive, tree-shaded shopping village is a pleasant place to browse. It boasts some 60 boutiques, gift and cook shops, as well as restaurants and a cinema.

✉ **Swann and Dakota Avenues** ☎ 813/251 3500

West Shore Plaza

Tampa's top fashion mall offers a wide selection of men's and women's clothing, accessories, children's clothes, and an FAO Schwartz toy store, plus three department stores, restaurants, and a food court.

✉ **Westshore and Kennedy Boulevards** ☎ 813/286 0790

Walt Disney World

Downtown Disney Marketplace

Home to a selection of souvenir and gift shops, but most importantly the vast and dangerously tempting World of Disney, the largest Disney merchandise store on the planet.

✉ **Buena Vista Drive, Lake Buena Vista** ☎ 407/828 3058

Northern Florida

Daytona

Beach Street

The restored historic storefronts along downtown Beach Street harbor a collection of specialty shops from antique collectibles to the Angell & Phelps Chocolate Factory (tours and free samples).

Jacksonville

Jacksonville Landing

A downtown landmark on the north bank of the St. Johns River, the Landing combines around 65 boutiques, gift shops, and specialty stores with a food court and several restaurants.

✉ **2 Independent Drive** ☎ 904/353 1188

Panama City Beach

Panama City Mall

This shopping, dining, and entertainment complex has more than 90 stores anchored by three department stores, plus a food court, movie theater and family games room.

✉ **2150 Martin Luther King Jr Boulevard** ☎ 850/785 9587

Pensacola

Cordova Mall

Pensacola's premier shopping center combines more than 140 fashion outlets, specialty shops and restaurants with a selection of department stores including Dillard's, Gayfers, and Montgomery Ward.

✉ **5100 N 9th Avenue at Bayou Boulevard** ☎ 850/477 5563

Tallahassee

Governor's Square

This popular shopping center provides a wide selection of fashion, sportswear, books, music and gifts, restaurants, and four department stores conveniently close to downtown.

✉ **1500 Apalachee Parkway** ☎ 850/671 INFO

Discount Outlets & Bargain Stores

Southern Florida and the Florida Keys

Florida City
Prime Outlets at Florida City
South of Miami, 45 factory outlet stores offering 25 to 75 percent off retail prices on Levis, Nike footwear, OshKosh B'Gosh, and more. There is also a food court and children's playground.
✉ 250 E Palm Drive (off US1 and Florida Turnpike)
☎ 305/248 4727

Fort Lauderdale
Sawgrass Mills
West of the Florida Turnpike, the world's largest discount outlet mall; 300 brand-name and designer stores include Neiman Marcus Last Call and Sak's off Fifth Avenue.
✉ W Sunrise Boulevard at Flamingo Road, Sunrise
☎ 954/846 2350

Fort Myers
Tanger Sanibel Factory Outlet Stores
Just east of the Sanibel Causeway, this mainland outlet mall offers bargain prices on clothing, footwear, and accessories.
✉ 20350 Summerlin Road
☎ 239/454 1974

Central Florida

Ellenton
Prime Outlets Ellenton
Just south of Tampa Bay, this is one of the largest factory outlet malls on the Gulf coast. More than 135 designer and name-brand stores.
✉ 5461 Factory Shops Boulevard (I-75/Exit 43) ☎ 941/723 1150 or 1-888 260 7608

Orlando
Belz Factory Outlet World
(▶ panel)
✉ 5401 W Oakridge Road
☎ 407/352 9611

Lake Buena Vista Factory Stores
Over 30 factory-direct outlet stores close to Walt Disney World Resort. Get 20 to 75 percent discounts on sportswear, jeans, and much more.
✉ 15591 S Apopka-Vineland Road/SR535
☎ 407/238 9301

Orlando Premium Outlets
Mall just off south I-Drive featuring designer names including Ralph Lauren, Giorgio Armani, Ferragamo, and Hugo Boss at bargain prices
✉ 8200 Vineland Avenue
☎ 407/238 7787

Northern Florida

Daytona
Daytona Flea and Farmer's Market
This sprawling 40-acre spread of booths and stalls, selling anything and everything from clothing to bric-à-brac at bargain prices, is a popular weekend (Fri–Sun) excursion.
✉ 2987 Bellevue Avenue
☎ 386/253 3330

St. Augustine
St. Augustine Outlet Center
Take advantage of discounts ranging from 25 to 75 percent on a wide selection of fashions, children's clothing, footwear, accessories, and toys from 90-plus outlet stores at this extensive mall.
✉ I-95/Exit 95 at SR16
☎ 904/825 1555

Bargain Belz
For shopaholics, the vast Belz Factory Shopping World in Orlando exercises all the inexorable pull of a major theme park. There are two full-scale malls and four annexes, containing 170 outlet stores offering a staggering range of discounted clothing, footwear, sporting goods, cosmetics, toys and accessories. And that is not all. Along with the Belz, the top end of International Drive is awash with bargains, from fashions at the International Designer Outlet Mall to Disney Gifts at the Quality Outlet Center.

Water Parks, Zoos &
Museums

Traveling with Children

Florida is probably the ultimate child-friendly vacation destination, but a couple of advance preparations can make your trip even more enjoyable—and safer. If you need child seats in your rented car, be sure to reserve them in advance. Hotels will provide cribs, but these also are best reserved ahead. High-factor sunblock is a must for all children and can be purchased at any supermarket or drugstore. Sun hats are a good idea, and make sure children get plenty to drink in the heat.

Miami

Miccosukee Indian Village and Airboat Tours

A half-day excursion out toward the northern entrance to the Everglades National Park at Shark Valley (▶ 41). Touristy alligator wrestling and Seminole Indian crafts, but the Everglades airboat rides are fun.

⊠ Tamiami Trail/US41 (30 miles W of downtown)
☎ 305/223 8380 ⏲ Daily 9–5

Southern Florida and the Florida Keys

Fort Lauderdale
Butterfly World

To the west of town, thousands of brightly colored butterflies flutter about the giant tropical aviaries at this popular attraction. There is also a hummingbird aviary and a museum of bugs and insects.

⊠ 3600 W Sample Road (I-95/Exit 36), Coconut Creek
☎ 954/977 4434 ⏲ Mon–Sat 9–5, Sun 1–5

Naples
Teddy Bear Museum

Over 3,000 toy and ornamental bears of all sizes and descriptions inhabit this cutesy museum in the woods. There is bear art, bear dioramas, Saturday morning bear story readings, and the inevitable bear gift shop.

⊠ 2511 Pine Ridge Road
☎ 239/598 2711 ⏲ Tue–Sat 10–5

West Palm Beach
Palm Beach Zoo at Dreher Park

A very good small zoo with plenty of shade. Highlights include endangered Florida panthers, and children are always delighted by the woolly llamas and lumbering giant tortoises.

⊠ 1301 Summit Boulevard
☎ 561/547 9453
⏲ Daily 9–5

Central Florida

Kissimmee
Green Meadows Petting Farm

A real treat for little children, who can find the theme parks quite overwhelming. In a shady farmyard setting, they can experience animal encounters with calves, lambs, ducklings, and ponies. Picnickers welcome.

⊠ 1368 S Poinciana Boulevard
☎ 407/846 0770 ⏲ Daily 9:30–5:30 (last tour at 4)

Water Mania

Water park with slides, pools, and water streams for a varied experience from gentle to dramatic.

⊠ 6073 West Irlo Bronson Memorial Highway
☎ 407/396 2626 ⏲ Daily Mar–Oct from 10AM, closing times from 5PM

Orlando
Wet 'n' Wild

Twenty-five acres of watery fun at the best water park in the area outside Walt Disney World Resort. Tackle some of the highest and fastest speed slides in the world, or take a gentle tube ride down the Lazy River. Kiddie pools and sunbathing decks.

⊠ 6200 International Drive
☎ 407/351 1800 or 1-800 992 9453 ⏲ Daily from 9 in summer, 10 in winter. Call for schedules

Space Coast
American Police Hall of Fame
Gory displays on crime and punishment, the chance to play detective and assorted gangster memorabilia will appeal particularly to older children.

✉ 6350 Horizon Drive, Titusville
☎ 321/264 0911 🕐 Daily 10–5:30

US Astronaut Hall of Fame
Just along from the Kennedy Space Center (▶ 17), the Hall of Fame offers an exciting and accessible array of space exhibits, "hands-on" displays, and stomach-churning simulator rides, plus a rather gentler ride in a full-scale mock-up of a space orbiter.

✉ 6225 Vectorspace Boulevard/SR405, Titusville
☎ 321/867 5000 🕐 Daily 9–5

Tampa
Lowry Park Zoo
It is not just the small-scale inhabitants of the Children's Village (including pygmy goats and Vietnamese pot-bellied piglets) that will appeal here. The Manatee and Aquatic Center and the Discovery Centers' Insect Zoo are big favorites.

✉ 1101 West Sligh Avenue
☎ 813/935 8552 🕐 Daily 9:30–5 (extended in summer)

Northern Florida

Jacksonville Beaches
Adventure Landing
A pirate-themed summer season water park is the main attraction here. Children can also let swing in the baseball batting cages, play miniature golf and race go-karts. On rainy days, there are indoor laser tag and arcade games.

✉ 2 Independent Drive
☎ 904/353 1188 🕐 Mon–Thu 3–9, Fri/Sat 3–midnight, Sun 12–9

Panama City Beach
Junior Museum of Bay County
A low-key attraction for younger children, this small museum adopts a "hands-on" approach to science, art, and nature exhibits. There are games in a life-size teepee, and chickens and ducks to feed in a re-created pioneer homestead.

✉ 1731 Jenks Avenue, Panama City ☎ 850/769 6128 🕐 Mon–Fri 9–4:30, Sat 10–4

Shipwreck Island Water Park
Six acres of watery thrills and spills, lazy inner tube rides, and speed slides. Little children are kept busy in the Tadpole Hole play area, and there are sunbathing decks and restaurants.

✉ 12000 Front Beach Road
☎ 850/234 0368 🕐 Jun–Labor Day 10:30–5:30; reduced hours Apr–May and Sep (call for schedules). Closed Oct–Mar

St. Augustine
St. Augustine Alligator Farm and Zoological Park
When the children have had their fill of history, cross the bay to Anastasia Island and take them to the World's Original Alligator Farm founded in 1893. Twenty three species of crocodilians, plus bird shows, and farm animals in the petting zoo.

✉ 999 Anastasia Boulevard (A1A) ☎ 904/824 3337
🕐 Daily 9–5

Theme Park Survival
The chief rule is don't overdo it. Young children in particular can find the major theme parks overwhelming and it is best to tailor your visit to their energy levels. Rent a stroller so little children can always hitch a ride, and take plenty of short breaks. Make sure young children carry some form of identification, such as a wrist tag, in case they get lost. And be warned: many of the more extreme thrill rides are limited to passengers measuring 44 inches or taller.

Sporting Activities

Ocean Reafforestation
Pollution, careless boaters and divers have taken a heavy toll on areas of Florida's natural coral reef. In addition to strict controls, one way of addressing the problem has been the introduction of artificial reef sites at depths between 15 and 400ft. This deliberate "ocean reafforestation" program has been a runaway success, creating healthy aquatic communities with an exciting variety of fish and other marine creatures and even new coral growth, both on the artificial sites and around sections of rejuvenated natural reef.

Canoeing and Kayaking
Florida's rivers and back bays offer a wealth of canoeing opportunities from a couple of hours' gentle wading in a state park to a backcountry marathon along the 99-mile Wilderness Waterway, which traverses the Everglades between Flamingo and Everglades City. Most state parks with a suitable stretch of river or waterfront have canoes for rent. Private tour and rental operations abound in prime canoeing areas like the Florida Keys, the Gulf islands, and the Panhandle. The following is a short list of top self-guided canoeing trails and tour operators:

Miami

Miami Beach
Urban Trails Kayak
⊠ Haulover Park, 10800 Collins Avenue ☎ 305/947 1302

Southern Florida and the Florida Keys

Everglades City
Everglades Rentals & Eco Adventures
⊠ 107 Camilla Street
☎ 239/695 3299

Key West
Mosquito Coast Island Outfitters
⊠ 1107 Duval Street
☎ 305/294 7178

Sanibel and Captiva Islands
Tarpon Bay Recreation Inc
⊠ 900 Tarpon Bay Road (off Sanibel-Captiva Road near J N "Ding" Darling Wildlife Refuge), Sanibel ☎ 941/472 8900

Central Florida

Ocala National Forest
Juniper Creek Canoe Run
⊠ Juniper Springs Recreation Area, SR40 ☎ 352/625 2808

Northern Florida

Milton
Blackwater River State Park
Blackwater Canoe Rental
⊠ 7720 Deaton Bridge Road, Milton ☎ 850/983 5363

Adventures Unlimited Outdoor Center
⊠ Tomahawk Landing, SR87 (12 miles N of Milton)
☎ 850/626 1669

Cycling
Florida is as flat as a pancake and provides no challenges for the serious mountain biker, but it can be fun for a gentle spin. Bike rental is readily available in many resorts. There is a bicycle trail around Palm Beach (➤ 21), the 47-mile Pinellas Trail in the Pinellas Suncoast area (➤ 63), and miles of bicycle paths in quieter spots such as Sanibel and Captiva Islands (➤ 24). Two bicycle trails in northern Florida are the 16-mile Tallahassee-St. Marks Historic Railroad Trail which starts 4 miles south of Tallahassee on SR363; and the 17-mile Gainesville–Hawthorne State Trail, which crosses Payne's Prairie State Preserve.

Diving and Snorkeling
Coral reefs, wrecks, artificial reef sites, and freshwater springs provide a terrific variety of diving and snorkeling experiences in

destinations throughout the state. Anyone can snorkel off the beach or in Florida's pure freshwater springs, such as Blue Spring (➤ 53), and Wakulla Springs (➤ 89).

In the Florida Keys and the southeast a large number of dive operators offer instruction, equipment renta,l and trips for snorkelers and certified divers to North America's only living coral reef, which stretches for 220 miles just off the Atlantic coast. The Gold Coast resorts of Fort Lauderdale and Palm Beach also boast a number of man-made reef sites fashioned from scuppered ships, bridge spans, and oil platforms (➤ 110, panel). The main Gulf coast dive centers are Panama City Beach and the Emerald Coast in Northern Florida. Below is a small selection of local operators.

Miami

Biscayne National Park Tours
✉ Convoy Point, 9700 SW 328th Street, Homestead
☎ 305/230 1100

South Beach Divers
✉ 850 Washington Avenue, Miami Beach ☎ 305/531 6110

Southern Florida and the Florida Keys

Fort Lauderdale
Pro Dive
✉ 515 Seabreeze Boulevard/A1A ☎ 954/776 3483

Islamorada
Bud n' Mary's Dive Center
✉ Mile Marker 79.8
☎ 305/664 2211

Key Largo
John Pennekamp Coral Reef State Park Dive Shop
✉ Mile Marker 102.5
☎ 305/451 6322

Lower Keys
Looe Key National Marine Sanctuary Dive Center
✉ Mile Marker 27.5, Ramrod Key ☎ 305/872 2215

West Palm Beach
Seapro Dive Center
✉ 3619 Broadway ☎ 561/844 3483

Northern Florida

Bradenton
Scuba Tech
✉ 826 13th Street W
☎ 941/746 5039

Panama City Beach
Hydrospace Dive Shop
✉ Hathaway Marina, 6422 W Highway 98 ☎ 850/234 3063

Fishing
Freshwater fishing on lakes and rivers and saltwater fishing from piers, bridges, and off the beach itself is a way of life in Florida. Fishermen over 16 may require state fishing licenses, which can be bought at any of the bait-and-tackle shops.

The rich Gulf of Mexico fishing grounds, and the Gulf Stream off the Atlantic coast spell huge rewards for deep-sea sport fishermen. The Atlantic sailfish, marlin, tarpon, amberjack, bonito, grouper, snapper, and pompano are among the prize catches pursued by charter fishing vessels from the Florida Keys to Fort Lauderdale, and from the Panhandle fishing centers of Destin and Fort Walton.

Ranger Programs
A great way to get a real insight into local flora, fauna, and history is to check out the ranger programs offered by many state and national parks. Ranger-led bird-watching and nature walks reveal all sorts of interesting snippets of information, and you can be sure the ranger's practiced eye will catch details that are easy to miss. During the winter high season, several parks host evening campfire programs, which are a big hit with children.

Across the State by Boat

Strange but true, you can cruise around most of Florida without ever hitting the open sea. Florida's Intracoastal Waterway is one of the world's most traveled water highways. It runs down the Atlantic coast from Fernandina Beach to Miami, protected from the open sea by a chain of barrier islands. A 150-mile section cuts across the state from Stuart on the Atlantic to Fort Myers on the Gulf of Mexico, where the barrier islands pick up again and accompany the route most of the way around to Pensacola.

Golf

There are over 1,100 golf courses in the state, many of championship standard. Some of the finest are operated by resort hotels, and many Florida hotels offer good value golfing packages. The cooler winter months are the best; during summer it is advisable to play early in the day to avoid the worst of the heat and afternoon showers. Top destinations include the Gold Coast, Naples, Orlando and Walt Disney World, and Ponte Vedra Beach near Jacksonville. A complete guide to Florida's private and public courses *Fairways in the Sunshine* is available from:

**Florida Sports Foundation
2930 Kerry Forest Parkway,
Tallahassee, FL 32308-2000
☎ 850/488 8347**

Hiking

Florida has over 60 state and national parks and forests, which provide a wealth of unspoiled hiking territory. Most offer a choice of short, well-marked nature trails and longer-distance hiking paths. Beach preserves, such as the Canaveral National Seashore and the Gulf Islands National Seashore in the Panhandle, are also wonderful for walking. For overnight camping trips backcountry hiking permits must be obtained from ranger stations. Mosquitoes can be a problem even on short excursions, so be sure to carry a good repellent, and take plenty of water.

Tennis

There are more than 7,700 tennis facilities across the state. As well as municipal facilities and full-time tennis camps, many hotels have courts, and several major sporting resort hotels offer tennis packages with coaching. For a full listing, contact:

**USTA (Florida Section)
1280 SW 36th Avenue, Pompano Beach, FL 33069 ☎ 954/968 3434**

Watersports

Windsurfing, waterskiing, jetskiing, and dinghy sailing are all popular pastimes around Florida's coast. Hotel watersports clubs and beachfront concessions rent out equipment. Determined surfers can try their luck on the Atlantic coast, but the waves are pretty tame. Central Florida's lakes are also popular for waterskiing.

If you rent a motorboat or a jetski keep a sharp lookout for Manatee Zones and cut your speed where requested.

Dolphin Encounters

While this is not exactly a sport, swimming with dolphins is very popular. Several organizations in the Florida Keys offer dolphin encounters, but book well in advance:

Marathon
**The Dolphin Connection
☎ 305/743 7000**

Key Largo
**Dolphins Plus
☎ 305/451 1993**

Grassy Key
**Dolphin Research Center
☎ 305/289 1121**

Orlando
**Discovery Cove
☎ 407/370 1280**

Spectator Sports

Football

Florida has three National Football League (NFL) teams who are based in Miami, Jacksonville, and Tampa.

Jacksonville Jaguars
✉ 1 Alltel Stadium Place
☎ 904/633 6050

Miami Dolphins
✉ Pro Player Stadium, 2269 Dan Marino Boulevard
☎ 954/452 7000

Tampa Bay Buccaneers
✉ 4201 N Dale Mabry Highway
☎ 813/879 BUCS

Baseball

Florida's two major league baseball teams are the Florida Marlins based in Miami and the Tampa Bay Devil Rays based in St. Petersburg. In addition, spring training (Feb–Apr) brings other opportunities (► panel).

Florida Marlins
✉ Pro Player Stadium, 2267 Dan Marino Boulevard
☎ 305/626 7400

The Tampa Bay Devil Rays
✉ Tropicana Field, 1 Tropicana Drive, St Petersburg
☎ 888/326 7297

Basketball

Florida's most successful basketball teams are based in Orlando and Miami.

Miami Heat
✉ American Airlines Arena, 601 Biscayne Boulevard
☎ 786/777 4328

Orlando Magic
✉ 8701 Maitland Summit Boulevard
☎ 407/916 2643

Golf

Championship courses host dozens of golfing events every year, including some PGA events. Contact:
PGA Tour
✉ 112 TPC Boulevard, Ponte Vedra Beach, FL 32082
☎ 904/285 3700

Car Racing

The top local events are the Marlboro Grand Prix of Miami at Homestead-Miami Speedway (Feb) and the Daytona 500 and Speed Weeks (Feb).

Daytona International Speedway
✉ 1801 W International Speedway Boulevard
☎ 904/253 RACE

Homestead-Miami Speedway
✉ 1 Speedway Boulevard
☎ 305/230 7223

Polo

World-class and championship matches (Dec–Apr).

Palm Beach Polo, Golf and Country Club
✉ 11199 Polo Club Road, Wellington ☎ 561/798 7000

Tennis

Tennis has a huge following in Florida. Watch the world's top players compete in these major local tournaments:

Bausch & Lomb Women's Championships (Apr)
✉ Amelia Island Plantation
☎ 1-800 486 8366

Nasdaq-100 Tournament (Mar)
✉ Tennis Center at Crandon Park, Key Biscayne (Miami)
☎ 305/442 3367

Spring Training

More than three-quarters of the nation's major league baseball teams gather in Florida for spring training. The highest concentration of visiting teams is found in the central Florida region, where cities such as Kissimmee, Clearwater and Tampa, as well as Walt Disney World itself, welcome the likes of the Houston Astros, Philadelphia Phillies, and New York Yankees. Training games are played as part of the Grapefruit League, tickets are cheap, and the action is fast and furious.

Nightlife

Nightclubbing

There are nightclubs in all Florida's major cities, but the most dynamic and impressive scene is (not surprisingly) Miami Beach's SoBe district. A cover charge should not cost more than about $15, except for multivenue complexes such as Walt Disney World's Pleasure Island (nearer $20). In line with Florida's drinking laws, most nightclubs will refuse entry to guests under 21, which is a major disappointment for many overseas visitors. It is advisable to carry a passport or some other proof of age.

Miami

Café Nostalgia
A taste of pre-Revolutionary hedonism, live Cuban music and lashings of nostalgia in Little Havana.
✉ 2212 SW 8th Street
☎ 305/541 2631 🕐 Thu–Sun 9PM–3AM

Clevelander
A bar and Ocean Drive landmark with exceptional people-watching potential.
✉ 1020 Ocean Drive, Miami Beach ☎ 305/531 3485
🕐 Nightly until 5AM

Club Deep
Has a 2,000-gallon aquarium underneath the dance floor. Dance and Latin music.
✉ 621 Washington Ave ☎ 305/532 1509 🕐 Nightly 10–5

Club Tropigala
Big-production, heavily besequinned musical revues to delight those who appreciate the full-on Las Vegas showtime approach.
✉ Fontainebleau Hilton, 4441 Collins Avenue, Miami Beach ☎ 305/672 7469 🕐 Nightly

The Improv
Miami's comedy showcase for the established and not-so-established.
✉ 3390 Mary St ☎ 305/441 8200 🕐 Tue–Sun

Jazid
This cool jazz venue in SoBe is just the place to simmer away on a tropical evening.
✉ 1342 Washington Avenue, Miami Beach ☎ 305/673 9372
🕐 Nightly

Opium
Three different areas to enjoy the latest dance tunes.

Currently a hot spot for the "in crowd."
✉ 136 Collins Avenue ☎ 305/531 5535 🕐 Tue and Thu–Sun 10–5

Tobacco Road
Historic live blues venue in the heart of the downtown district, which also features regular jazz nights.
✉ 626 S Miami Avenue ☎ 305/374 1198 🕐 Nightly until 5AM

Van Dyke Café
Upstairs at the Van Dyke offers a great café-restaurant setting for some of the best jazz acts around plus blues and Latin American sounds.
✉ 846 Linclon Road, Miami Beach ☎ 305/534 3600
🕐 Nightly

Southern Florida and the Florida Keys

Fort Lauderdale
O'Hara's Pub
One of the top live jazz venues in the southeast. Also Sunday lunchtime sessions.
✉ 722 E Las Olas Boulevard ☎ 954/524 1764 🕐 Nightly

Key West
Rick's
Popular nightspot with live music downstairs and dancing in the Upstairs Bar.
✉ 202 Duval Street ☎ 305/296 5513 🕐 Café until 11PM; bar 8PM–4AM

West Palm Beach
Respectable Street Café
Progressive nightclub in the downtown entertainment and dining district. Theme nights from techno and rave to retro.
✉ 518 Clematis Street

☎ 561/832 9999 ⏰ Tue–Sat from 9PM

Central Florida

Orlando
CityWalk
Over 40 restaurants, bars, clubs, a stage for live music, and a multiplex cinema make CityWalk an atmospheric place. Pay homage to reggae at Bob Marley—A Tribute to Freedom and enjoy a touch of downtown New Orleans at Pat O'Brien's Orlando. Age restrictions apply at some venues.
✉ Universal Studios, Universal Boulevard ☎ 407/363 8000

Metropolis and Matrix
A twin venue with Metropolis providing a sophisticated club atmosphere while the special effects and a multi-million dollar light show at Matrix make this one of the best places to groove.
✉ Pointe*Orlando, 9101 International Drive ☎ 407/370 3700

Tampa
Green Iguana
A choice of bars, live bands, early evening jazz sessions at the heart of the Ybor City nightlife district.
✉ 1708 E 7th Avenue, Ybor City ☎ 813/248 9555

Walt Disney World
Downtown Disney Pleasure Island
A one-off admission fee covers entry to high-energy, 1970s retro and rock and roll discotheques, comedy and jazz clubs, plus an Old West-themed saloon bar.
✉ Downtown Disney, E Buena Vista Drive ☎ 407/934 7781
⏰ Nightly until 2AM

Northern Florida

Daytona Beach
Razzle's
Dramatic light shows accompany chart and progressive sounds.
✉ 611 Seabreeze Boulevard ☎ 904/257 6236 ⏰ Daily 8PM–3AM

Pensacola
Sluggo's
Three floors of bars, books, games, pool tables, and live music at this distinctly wacky but hugely entertaining downtown venue.
✉ 130 Palafox Street ☎ 850/435 0543 ⏰ Tue–Sun 3PM–3AM

Dinner Shows
Themed dinner shows make great entertainment for the whole family.

Arabian Nights
A glittering equestrian spectacular.
✉ 6225 West Irlo Bronson Memorial Highway, Kissimmee ☎ 407/239 9223

Dolly Parton's Dixie Stampede
A southern "ho-down."
✉ 8251 Vineland Ave, Orlando ☎ 407/238 2777

Medieval Times
Daring do by knights of old.
✉ 4510 West Irlo Bronson Memorial Highway, Kissimmee ☎ 407/239 0214

Pirate's Dinner Adventure
Swashbuckling adventure on the high seas.
✉ 6400 Carrier Drive, Orlando ☎ 407/248 0590

Bars and Cafés
Florida is well supplied with watering holes, from TV-lined sports bars and pub-style microbreweries to sidewalk cafés and poolside tiki bars (South Seas island theme and exotic cocktails). Most lure in the early evening crowd with cut-price drinks (usually two-for-the-price-of-one deals) during Happy Hour, which generally runs from 4PM–7PM, though this is a distinctly flexible arrangement. At night, many bars in cities and tourist areas metamorphose into live music venues with no cover charge.

What's On When

Theme Park Celebrations

Public holidays are a great excuse for central Florida's theme parks to break out the fireworks and party hats to celebrate in style. In spring, Universal Studios hosts a spectacular six-week Mardi Gras (Feb–Mar), and Walt Disney World Resort's Magic Kingdom holds an enormous Easter Sunday Parade. Fireworks and marching bands accompany the Independence Day celebrations, and the run-up to Halloween is another favorite, with special parties at SeaWorld as well as Disney's Magic Kingdom and Universal Studios. A few weeks later all the parks go to town for Christmas and New Year.

January

Art Deco Weekend (mid-Jan): Miami's Art Deco district hosts a street festival featuring period music, classic automobiles, and fashions.

February

Daytona Speed Weeks (first three weeks): car racing extravaganza.
Silver Spurs Rodeo (last weekend): cowboy skills on show in Kissimmee.

March

Annual Sanibel Shell Fair (first week): sea shell displays and crafts in America's top shelling spot.
Carnaval Miami (second weekend): the nation's biggest Hispanic festival with top entertainers and parades.
Florida Indian Association Pow Wow (last weekend). The largest Native American "get-together", at Fort Pierce, with singing, dancing, and art competitions.

April

Pompano Beach Seafood Festival (last weekend): seafood, live music, arts and crafts on the Gold Coast.
Jacksonville Jazz Festival (last weekend): free festival featuring a host of stars.

May

Florida Folk Festival: musicians gather at the Stephen Foster State Cultural Center in White Springs.
SunFest (first week): Florida's premier music, arts, and boating celebration in West Palm Beach.
Cajun/Zydeco Crawfish Festival (first weekend). Multiple soundstages at Fort Lauderdale offer live music plus gumbo, crawfish, and watermelon to sample.

June

Fiesta of Five Flags (early Jun): boat and street parades, sandcastle contest, and more in Pensacola.

July

Suncoast Offshore Grand Prix (Jun–Jul): regatta races, fishing tournaments, and entertainment culminating in the big race on Sarasota Bay.
Independence Day (Jul 4): celebrations throughout the state.

August

Venice Seafood Festival: seafood cooking competitions and boat exhibitions attract crowds to this beach town.

September

Las Olas Art Fair (early Sep): art sales, music and food along Fort Lauderdale's main shopping street.

October

Fantasy Fest (last week): Key West's Wild Halloween carnival with a distinctly Caribbean twist.

November

Amelia Heritage Festival (Thanksgiving–New Year): Civil War re-enactments and tours of Fernandina Beach's historic district.

December

Mickey"s Very Merry Christmas Party: festive celebrations at the Magic Kingdom in the Walt Disney World Resort (▶ panel).
Festival of Lights: a spectacular display at Silver Springs around Dec 12–27.

Practical Matters

Pedestrian and road signs are clear and self-explanatory

TIME DIFFERENCES

GMT	Most of Florida	The Panhandle	Germany	Netherlands	Spain
12 noon	7AM	6AM	1PM	1PM	1PM

BEFORE YOU GO

WHAT YOU NEED

- ● Required
- ○ Suggested
- ▲ Not required

Contact your travel agent or the U.S. embassy for the current regulations regarding passports and the Visa Waiver Form/Visa. Your passport should be valid for at lest six months beyond date of entry.

	UK	Germany	USA	Netherlands	Spain
Passport/National Identity Card (Valid for 6 months after entry)	●	●	▲	●	●
Visa Waiver Form	●	●	▲	●	●
Onward or Return Ticket	●	●	▲	●	●
Health Inoculations (tetanus)	○	○	○	○	○
Health Documentation (reciprocal agreement) (▶ 123, Health)	▲	▲	▲	▲	▲
Travel Insurance	●	●	▲	●	●
Driving Licence (national or International Driving Permit)	●	●	●	●	●
Car Insurance Certificate	○	○	●	○	○
Car Registration Document	●	●	●	●	●

WHEN TO GO

Central Florida/Orlando

High season
Low season

22°C	23°C	25°C	27°C	27°C	30°C	32°C	32°C	30°C	28°C	25°C	22°C
JAN	FEB	MAR	APR	MAY	JUN	JUL	AUG	SEP	OCT	NOV	DEC

☀ Sun   ☁ Cloud   🌧 Wet   ⛅ Sunshine and showers

TOURIST OFFICES

In the UK:
Visit Florida
c/o KBCPR
Suite 3, Falmer Court
London Road
Uckfield
East Sussex TN22 1HN
☎ 01825 763633

In the US:
Visit Florida
661 E Jefferson Street
Suite 300
Tallahassee
FL 32301
☎ 850/488 5607
www.flausa.com

WHEN YOU ARE THERE

ARRIVING

Most visitors to Florida arrive at the international airport gateways of Miami and Orlando. Some direct scheduled flights also arrive at Tampa, and charter flights to Sanford (for Orlando), Daytona, Fort Myers and Fort Lauderdale are increasingly popular. U.S. domestic airlines serve numerous local airports.

Miami International Airport	Journey times
Miles to Miami Beach	

10 miles

	N/A
	30 minutes
	25 minutes

Orlando International Airport	Journey times
Miles to city centre	

9¼ miles

	N/A
	45 minutes
	30 minutes

MONEY

An unlimited amount of American dollars can be imported or exported, but amounts of over $10,000 must be reported to U.S. Customs. U.S. traveler's checks are accepted as cash in most places (not taxis) as are credit cards (Amex, Visa, Access, Mastercard, Diners).

Dollar bills come in 1, 2, 5, 10, 20, 50 and 100 denominations. Note that all dollar bills are the same size and color—all greenbacks. One dollar is made up of 100 cents. Coins are of 1 cent (penny), 5 cents (nickel), 10 cents (dime), 25 cents (quarter), and one dollar.

TIME

Local time in Florida is Eastern Standard Time (GMT −5), with the exception of the Panhandle region, west of the Apalachicola River, which is on Central Standard Time (GMT −6). Daylight saving applies (Apr–Oct).

CUSTOMS

YES

There are duty-free allowances for non-U.S. residents over 21 years of age:

Alcohol: spirits (over 22% volume):	1L
Wine:	1L
Cigarettes:	200 or
Cigars:	50 or
Tobacco:	2kg
Duty-free gifts:	$100

provided the stay in the US is at least 72 hours and that gift exemption has not been claimed in the previous six months. There are no currency limits.

NO

Meat or meat products, dairy products, fruits, seeds, drugs, lottery tickets, or obscene publications. Never carry a bag through customs for anyone else.

CONSULATES

UK	**Germany**	**Netherlands**	**Spain**
☎ 305/374 1522	☎ 305/358 0290	☎ 786/866 0480	☎ 305/446 5511
(Miami)	(Miami)	(Miami)	(Miami)

WHEN YOU ARE THERE

TOURIST OFFICES

There are Local Visitor
Information Offices at:

Fort Lauderdale:
● 1850 Eller Drive, Suite 303
 ☎ 954/765 4466

Fort Myers (Sanibel and Captiva Islands)
● 1159 Causeway Boulevard,
 Sanibel
 ☎ 941/472 1080

Key West:
● 402 Wall Street
 ☎ 305/294 2587

Miami:
● 701 Brickell Avenue,
 Suite 2700
 ☎ 305/539 3000 and
 800/933 8448

Orlando:
● 8723 International Drive,
 Suite 101
 ☎ 407/363 5872

Palm Beach:
● 45 Coconut Row
 ☎ 561/655 3282

Pensacola:
● 1401 E Gregory Street
 ☎ 850/434 1234

St. Augustine:
● 88 Riberia Street
 ☎ 904/829 1711

St. Petersburg:
● 14450 46th Street N
 ☎ 727/464 7200

Sarasota:
● 655 N Tamiami Trail
 ☎ 941/957 1877

NATIONAL HOLIDAYS

J	F	M	A	M	J	J	A	S	O	N	D
2	1	(1)	(1)	1		1		1	2	2	2

1 Jan	New Year's Day
Jan (third Mon)	Martin Luther King Day
Feb (third Mon)	President's Day
Mar/Apr	Good Friday
May (last Mon)	Memorial Day
4 July	Independence Day
Sep (first Mon)	Labor Day
Oct (second Mon)	Columbus Day
11 Nov	Veterans' Day
Nov (fourth Thu)	Thanksgiving
25 Dec	Christmas Day

Boxing Day is not a public holiday in the U.S. Some
shops open on National Holidays.

OPENING HOURS

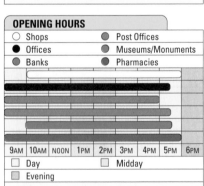

○ Shops	● Post Offices
● Offices	● Museums/Monuments
● Banks	● Pharmacies

9AM	10AM	NOON	1PM	2PM	3PM	4PM	5PM	6PM

□ Day	□ Midday
□ Evening	

Shopping malls stay open until 9PM or later during the
week, and many open on Sundays from around 11–5.
Stores in resort areas may also keep more flexible
hours. Post offices are not always easy to find and
are closed on Saturdays; hotels will often help with
basic postal needs. Theme park opening hours vary
seasonally. Museum hours also vary; many close on
Mondays, but stay open late one night a week. There
are 24-hour pharmacies in all major towns; details
will be posted at other pharmacies.

DRIVE ON THE RIGHT

RESTROOMS FREE

★ ★
★ ☆

PUBLIC TRANSPORTATION

 Air U.S. domestic carriers serve local airports in all Florida's major cities and vacation destinations. International airports such as Orlando receive direct flights from around 70 different U.S. destinations. Domestic APEX airfares are very reasonable and it is well worth shopping around for good deals.

 Trains Daily Amtrak (☎ 1-800/USA RAIL) services from Washington D.C. arrive the following day at Orlando (22 hours), Miami (27 hours), and Tampa (28 hours). The overnight AutoTrain service carries cars and passengers from Lorton, VA to Sanford (for Orlando). There is also a tri-weekly cross-country service from Los Angeles via the Panhandle for Miami. Train services within Florida are very limited; visitors to the southeast can use the inexpensive Tri-Rail commuter network which links Miami and West Palm Beach via Fort Lauderdale and Boca Raton.

 Buses Greyhound buses provide a fairly comprehensive network of routes linking Florida's main cities and towns (☎ 1-800/229 9424). Passes for unlimited travel from four to 60 days are best purchased overseas, though savings are available on advance purchase tickets within the U.S. Local bus services are infrequent.

 Urban Transportation Door-to-door airport shuttle bus services to downtown and resort areas are a cheap and convenient alternative to taxis. Urban bus routes are generally geared toward commuters, although Orlando is well served by Lynx buses and the I-Ride service along International Drive. In Miami, some Metrobus services can be used for sightseeing; downtown is served by the elevated Metromover light rail link; and there are Metrorail connections to Coconut Grove and Coral Gables.

CAR RENTAL

 The best way to get around in Florida. Rates are very competitive. Take an unlimited mileage deal, collision damage waiver, and adequate (more than minimal) insurance. There is a surcharge on drivers under 25 and the minimum age is often 21 (sometimes 25).

TAXIS

 Taxis ("cabs"), can be picked up from the airport or hotel or booked by telephone (see Yellow Pages). Rates are around \$2.80 for the first mile and around \$1.50 for each additional mile. Water taxi services are available in Miami, Fort Lauderdale, and Jacksonville.

DRIVING

 Speed limit on interstate highways: **55–70mph**

 Speed limit on main roads: **55–65mph**

 Speed limit on urban roads: **20–35mph**. All speed limits are strictly enforced.

 Seat belts must be worn by drivers and front seat passengers. Car seats are mandatory for under-threes; older children need a safety seat or seat belt.

 There are tough drinking and driving laws. Never drive under the influence of alcohol. Opened cans or bottles containing alcohol in cars are illegal.

 Gasoline (fuel) is cheaper in America than in Europe. It is sold in American gallons (five American gallons equal 18 litres) and comes in three grades, all unleaded. Many gas stations have automatic pumps that accept notes and major credit cards.

 If you break down pull over, raise the hood (bonnet), turn on the hazard lights and call the rental company or the breakdown number (on or near the dashboard). The American Automobile Association (AAA) provides certain reciprocal facilities to affiliated motoring organizations in other countries. For AAA breakdown assistance ☎ 1-800/222 4357 (toll free).

At top of page, a ruler scale:

CENTIMETRES 0 1 2 3 4 5 6 7 8

INCHES 0 1 2 3

PERSONAL SAFETY

Florida is not generally a dangerous place but to help prevent crime and accidents:

- Never open your hotel room door unless you know who is there. If in doubt call hotel security.
- Always lock your front and/or patio doors when sleeping in the room or going out. Use the safety chain/lock for security.
- When driving keep all car doors locked.
- If lost, stop in a well-lit gas station or ask for directions in a hotel, restaurant or shop.
- Never approach alligators, as they can outrun a man.

Police assistance:
☎ **091**
from any call box

TELEPHONES

Making telephone calls from hotel rooms is expensive. Public telephones are found in hotel lobbies, drugstores, restaurants, gas stations and at the roadside. A local call costs 25 cents. Dial "0" for the operator. To 'call collect' means to reverse the charges.

International Dialling Codes	
From Florida (US) to:	
UK:	**011 44**
Ireland:	**011 353**
Australia:	**011 61**
Germany:	**011 49**
Netherlands:	**011 31**
Spain:	**011 34**

POST

Post offices in Florida are few and far between. Vending machines sell stamps at a 25 percent premium; it is best to purchase them at their face value in your hotel. Post offices are usually open Mon–Fri 9–5; hotels and major attractions often provide postal services.

ELECTRICITY

The power supply is: 110/120 volts AC (60 cycles)

Type of socket:

 sockets take two-prong, flat-pin plugs. Visitors should bring adaptors for their three-pin and two-round-pin plugs. European visitors should bring a voltage transformer as well as an adapter.

TIPS/GRATUITIES

Yes ✓ No ✗		
It is useful to carry plenty of small notes		
Restaurants (if service not included)	✓	15–20%
Cafeterias/fast-food outlets	✗	
Bar Service	✓	15%
Taxis	✓	15%
Tour guides (discretionary)	✓	
Hotels (chambermaid/doorman etc)	✓	$1 per day
Porters	✓	$1 per bag
Hairdressers	✓	15%
Toilets (rest rooms)	✗	

PHOTOGRAPHY
What to photograph: Florida's colorful theme parks are great places to take pictures. There are plenty of opportunities to take good beach photos, and flora and fauna, too. Always protect cameras from sand and water.
When to photograph: avoid the glare of midday for the best results. Use a fast film (400ASA) for night-time shots.
Where to buy film: all types of film and photo processing are available in drug stores and theme parks.

HEALTH

Insurance
Medical insurance cover of at least $1,000,000 unlimited cover is strongly recommended, as medical bills can be astronomical and treatment may be withheld if you have no evidence of means to pay.

Dental Services
Your medical insurance cover should include dental treatment, which is readily available, but expensive. Have a check-up before you go. Dental referral telephone numbers are in the Yellow Pages telephone directory or ask at your hotel.

Sun Advice
By far the most common cause of ill health among visitors to Florida is too much sun. Use sunscreen on the beach and when sightseeing. Ensure that everyone drinks plenty of fluids. For minor sunburn, aloe vera gel is very soothing.

Drugs
Medicines can be bought at drugstores, though certain drugs generally available elsewhere require a prescription in the U.S. Acetaminophen is the U.S. equivalent of paracetamol. Use an insect repellent containing DEET, and cover up after dark to avoid being bitten by mosquitoes.

Safe Water
Tap water is drinkable throughout Florida, though not particularly palatable. Mineral water is cheap and readily available. Restaurants usually provide customers with a pitcher of iced tap water.

CONCESSIONS

Students/Youths: Many sights and attractions offer special admission prices to students in possession of an International Student Identity Card. Children under three are generally allowed into attractions free; children's tickets are usually available up to age 12. Teenagers often have to pay the full adult rate.

Senior Citizens (Seniors): Florida offers special deals for senior citizens from discounted admission to museums and other sightseeing attractions to reduced room rates in hotels during the low season. Minimum age limits can vary, but many aged over 55 will qualify.

CLOTHING SIZES

Florida (USA)	UK	Rest of Europe	
36	36	46	
38	38	48	
40	40	50	
42	42	52	Suits
44	44	54	
46	46	56	
8	7	41	
8½	7½	42	
9½	8½	43	
10½	9½	44	Shoes
11½	10½	45	
12	11	46	
14½	14½	37	
15	15	38	
15½	15½	39/40	
16	16	41	Shirts
16½	16½	42	
17	17	43	
6	8	34	
8	10	36	
10	12	38	
12	14	40	Dresses
14	16	42	
16	18	44	
6	4½	38	
6½	5	38	
7	5½	39	
7½	6	39	Shoes
8	6½	40	
8½	7	41	

WHEN DEPARTING

- Allow plenty of time to reach the airport. Rental car depots are usually outside the airport and you will need to take a shuttle bus to the terminal.
- Check-in is at least three hours before departure time.
- Duty-free goods purchased at the airport are delivered to passengers at the door to the plane before take-off.

LANGUAGE

The official language of the U.S. is English, and, given that one third of all overseas visitors come from the U.K., Florida's natives have few problems coping with British accents and dialects. Hotel staff in larger tourist hotels may speak other European languages; Spanish is widely spoken, as many workers in the hotel and catering industries are of Latin American origin. However, many English words have different meanings in the U.S., below are some of the words most likely to cause confusion:

holiday	*vacation*	tap	*faucet*
fortnight	*two weeks*	rooms with	*efficiencies*
ground floor	*first floor*	cooking facilities	
first floor	*second floor*	luggage	*baggage*
flat	*apartment*	hotel porter	*bellhop*
holiday	*condominium,*	chambermaid	*room maid*
apartment	*condo*	surname	*last name*
lift	*elevator*	cupboard	*closet*

cheque	*check*	25 cent coin	*quarter*
travellers'	*travelers'*	banknote	*bill*
cheque	*check*	banknote	*greenback*
1 cent coin	*penny*	(colloquial)	
5 cent coin	*nickel*	dollar (colloquial)	*buck*
10 cent coin	*dime*	cashpoint	*automatic teller*

grilled	*broiled*	biscuit	*cookie*
frankfurter	*hot dog*	scone	*biscuit*
prawn	*shrimp*	sorbet	*sherbet*
aubergine	*eggplant*	jelly	*jello*
courgette	*zucchini*	jam	*jelly*
maize	*corn*	confectionery	*candy*
chips (potato)	*fries*	spirit	*liquor*
crisps (potato)	*chips*	soft drink	*soda*

car	*automobile*	petrol	*gas, gasoline*
bonnet (of car)	*hood*	railway	*railroad*
boot (of car)	*trunk*	tram	*streetcar*
repair	*fix*	underground	*subway*
caravan	*trailer*	platform	*track*
lorry	*truck*	buffer	*bumper*
motorway	*freeway*	single ticket	*one-way ticket*
main road	*highway*	return ticket	*round-trip ticket*

shop	*store*	nappy	*diaper*
chemist (shop)	*drugstore*	glasses	*eyeglasses*
bill (in a	*check*	policeman	*cop*
restaurant)		post	*mail*
cinema	*movie theater*	postcode	*zip code*
pavement	*sidewalk*	ring up,	*call*
subway	*underpass*	telephone	
gangway	*aisle*	long-distance	*trunk call*
toilet	*rest room*	call	
trousers	*pants*	autumn	*fall*

INDEX

Acknowledgements

The Automobile Association wishes to thank the following photographers, libraries and associations for their assistance in the preparation of this book.
© 1998 BUSCH GARDENS TAMPA BAY, INC. All rights reserved. 64b; © DISNEY ENTERPRISES, INC. 26b, 70, 71; MARY EVANS PICTURE LIBRARY 10b; HEMINGWAY HOUSE 14b; INTERNATIONAL SPEEDWAY CORPORATION 74/5; KENNEDY SPACE CENTER, FLORIDA 8b; MRI BANKER'S GUIDE TO FOREIGN CURRENCY 119; ORLANDO/ORANGE COUNTY CONVENTION AND VISITORS BUREAU 53
The remaining photographs are held in the Association's own photo library (AA PHOTO LIBRARY), the following were taken by: PETE BENNETT 5b, 6a, 6b, 7a, 8a, 9a, 9b, 9c, 10a, 11a, 12a, 13a, 13b, 13c, 14a, 17b, 22b, 28b, 37b, 45b, 51, 52a, 52b, 54, 55a, 55b, 56a, 56/7, 57, 58a, 59a, 59b, 60, 61b, 62a, 62b, 63, 64a, 65a, 66, 67, 68a, 68b, 72, 76, 77a, 78b, 79b, 80b, 81a, 82b, 82c, 83a, 84b, 85a, 86b, 87b, 88, 89; JON DAVISON 1, 20b, 27a, 28a, 29, 30, 31, 34a, 36, 37a; DAVID LYONS 7c, 16b, 33, 34b, 35; PAUL MURPHY B/cover Busch Gardens, 117b; LANNY PROVO 2, 5a, 38, 42b; TONY SOUTER 6c, 11b, 39, 42a, 45a, 46, 47a, 58b, 61a, 61c, 73, 83b, 91b; the remainder were taken by JAMES A TIMS.

Emma Stanford wishes to thank Tanya Nigro at Florida Tourism in London and the many regional tourist offices throughout Florida for their invaluable help.

Copy Editor: Penny Phenix   **Page Layout:** Barfoot Design   **Updated by:** Big World Productions
Revision Management: Pam Stagg

Dear Essential Traveller

**Your comments, opinions and recommendations are very
important to us. So please help us to improve our travel
guides by taking a few minutes to complete this simple
questionnaire.**

*You do not need a stamp (unless posted outside the UK). If you do not want to cut this page
from your guide, then photocopy it or write your answers on a plain sheet of paper.*

Send to: **The Editor, AA World Travel Guides,
FREEPOST SCE 4598, Basingstoke RG21 4GY.**

Your recommendations…

We always encourage readers' recommendations for restaurants, nightlife
or shopping – if your recommendation is used in the next edition of the
guide, we will send you a *FREE* AA *Essential* **Guide** of your choice.
Please state below the establishment name, location and your reasons
for recommending it.

_____

_____

_____

_____

Please send me **AA *Essential*** _____

About this guide…

Which title did you buy?
    AA *Essential* _____
Where did you buy it? _____
When? <u>m m</u> / <u>y y</u>

Why did you choose an AA *Essential* Guide? _____

_____

_____

_____

_____

Did this guide meet your expectations?
    Exceeded ☐   Met all ☐   Met most ☐   Fell below ☐
    Please give your reasons _____

_____

_____

_____

continued on next page…

Were there any aspects of this guide that you particularly liked? _____

_____

_____

Is there anything we could have done better? _____

_____

_____

About you...

Name (*Mr/Mrs/Ms*) _____

    Address _____

_____

_____ Postcode _____

    Daytime tel nos _____

Please only give us your mobile phone number if you wish to hear from us about other products and services from the AA and partners by text or mms.

Which age group are you in?
    Under 25 ☐   25–34 ☐   35–44 ☐   45–54 ☐   55–64 ☐   65+ ☐

How many trips do you make a year?
    Less than one ☐   One ☐   Two ☐   Three or more ☐

Are you an AA member? Yes ☐   No ☐

About your trip...

When did you book? m m / y y   When did you travel? m m / y y

How long did you stay? _____

Was it for business or leisure? _____

Did you buy any other travel guides for your trip?

    If yes, which ones? _____

Happy Holidays!

The Atlas

Acknowledgements
All pictures are from AA World Travel Library with contributions from the following photographers:
Jon Davison: volleyball on Miami's South Beach, Miami Seaquarium, the skies above Key West
Lanny Provo: airboat in the Everglades National Park
Tony Souter: skyscraper in downtown Orlando

www.theAA.com
The Automobile Association's website offers comprehensive up-to-the-minute information covering AA-approved hotels, guest houses and B&Bs, restaurants and pubs in the UK, along with airport parking, insurance, European breakdown cover, European motoring advice, a ferry planner, overseas fuel prices, a bookshop and much more.

www.aaa.com
AAA's website offers comprehensive information covering AAA-approved hotels and restaurants in the US. In addition, AAA can assist US citizens with obtaining a passport, reservations and tickets for cruise, tour, motorcoach, rail and air travel. AAA provides information on independent or escorted tours for individuals or groups and offers benefits on cruises, tours and travel packages.

The Foreign and Commonwealth Office
Country advice, traveller's tips, before you go information, checklists and more.
www.fco.gov.uk

Visit USA Association
www.visitusa.org.uk

GENERAL
UK Passport Service
www.ukpa.gov.uk

US passport information
www.travel.state.gov

Health Advice for Travellers
www.doh.gov.uk/traveladvice

BBC – Holiday
www.bbc.co.uk/holiday

The Full Universal Currency Converter
www.xe.com/ucc/full.shtml

Flying with Kids
www.flyingwithkids.com

The official portal of the State of Florida, with political and infrastructure information plus visitor attractions.
www.myflorida.com

All the latest gossip and information on the South Beach 'scene'.
www.southbeach-usa.com

Details about the flora and fauna of the Florida state parks and the activities you can enjoy there.
www.floridastateparks.org

Full listings of all Florida sporting competitions and recreational sports.
www.flasports.com

Comprehensive information to help you plan your trip to the world of Disney.
www.disneyworld.com

TRAVEL
Flights and information
www.cheapflights.co.uk
www.thisistravel.co.uk
www.ba.com
www.continental.com
www.worldairportguide.com

ATLAS SYMBOLS

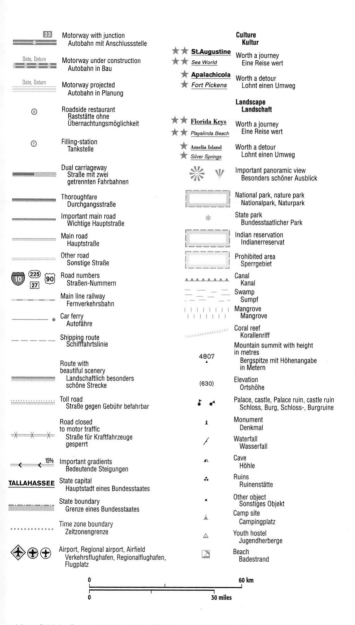

23	Motorway with junction Autobahn mit Anschlussstelle
Date, Datum	Motorway under construction Autobahn in Bau
Date, Datum	Motorway projected Autobahn in Planung
⑧	Roadside restaurant Raststätte ohne Übernachtungsmöglichkeit
⑦	Filling-station Tankstelle
	Dual carriageway Straße mit zwei getrennten Fahrbahnen
	Thoroughfare Durchgangsstraße
	Important main road Wichtige Hauptstraße
	Main road Hauptstraße
	Other road Sonstige Straße
10 225 27 90	Road numbers Straßen-Nummern
	Main line railway Fernverkehrsbahn
	Car ferry Autofähre
	Shipping route Schifffahrtslinie
	Route with beautiful scenery Landschaftlich besonders schöne Strecke
	Toll road Straße gegen Gebühr befahrbar
	Road closed to motor traffic Straße für Kraftfahrzeuge gesperrt
15%	Important gradients Bedeutende Steigungen
TALLAHASSEE	State capital Hauptstadt eines Bundesstaates
	State boundary Grenze eines Bundesstaates
	Time zone boundary Zeitzonengrenze
✈ ✈ ✈	Airport, Regional airport, Airfield Verkehrsflughafen, Regionalflughafen, Flugplatz

Culture
Kultur

★★ **St.Augustine**	Worth a journey
★★ *Sea World*	Eine Reise wert
★ **Apalachicola**	Worth a detour
★ *Fort Pickens*	Lohnt einen Umweg

Landscape
Landschaft

★★ **Florida Keys**	Worth a journey
★★ *Playalinda Beach*	Eine Reise wert
★ **Amelia Island**	Worth a detour
★ *Silver Springs*	Lohnt einen Umweg

☀ ⩔	Important panoramic view Besonders schöner Ausblick
	National park, nature park Nationalpark, Naturpark
✳	State park Bundesstaatlicher Park
	Indian reservation Indianerreservat
	Prohibited area Sperrgebiet
	Canal Kanal
	Swamp Sumpf
	Mangrove Mangrove
	Coral reef Korallenriff
4807 ▲	Mountain summit with height in metres Bergspitze mit Höhenangabe in Metern
(630)	Elevation Ortshöhe
♪ ♪	Palace, castle, Palace ruin, castle ruin Schloss, Burg, Schloss-, Burgruine
⚑	Monument Denkmal
∕	Waterfall Wasserfall
⌒	Cave Höhle
⁂	Ruins Ruinenstätte
▪	Other object Sonstiges Objekt
⚐	Camp site Campingplatz
△	Youth hostel Jugendherberge
▨	Beach Badestrand

0   60 km
0   30 miles

Maps © Mairs Geographischer Verlag / Falk Verlag, 73751 Ostfildern

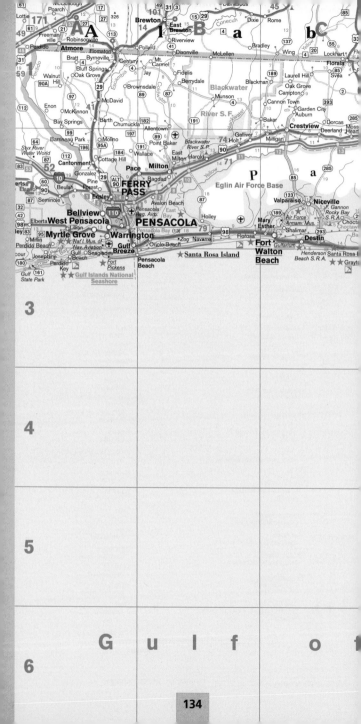

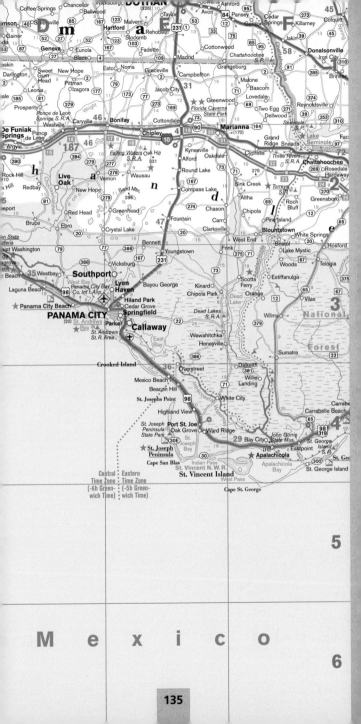

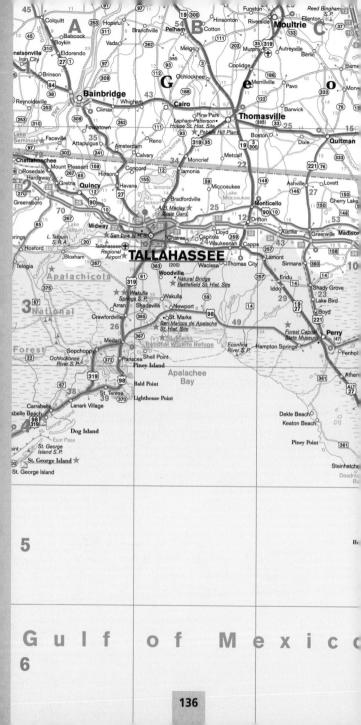

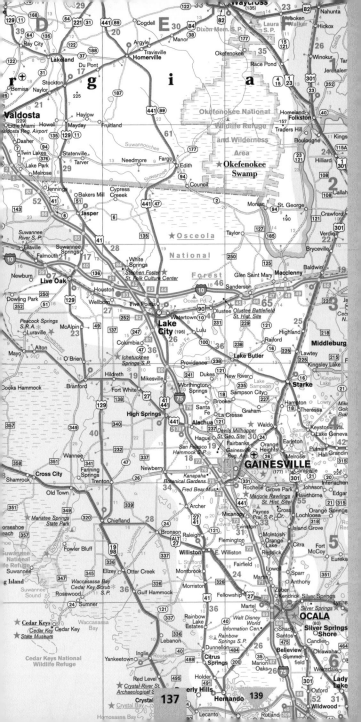

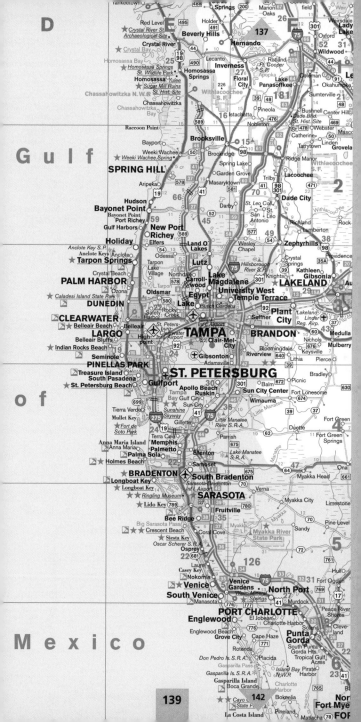

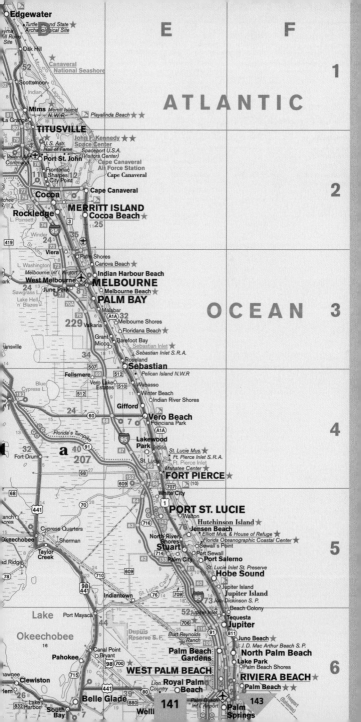

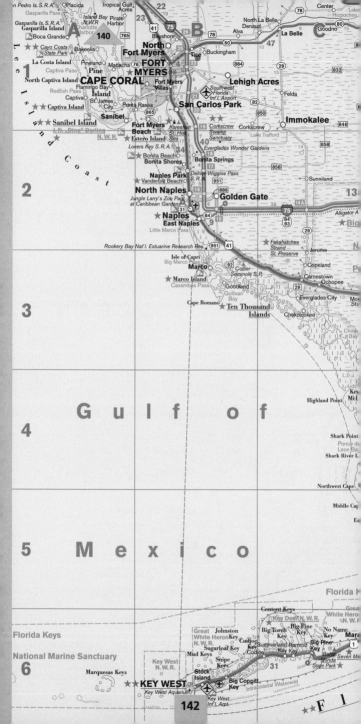